SpringerBriefs in Population Studies

Volume 2

AF866986

For further volumes:
http://www.springer.com/series/10047

Dean H. Judson · David A. Swanson

Estimating Characteristics of the Foreign Born by Legal Status

An Evaluation of Data and Methods

Springer

Dean H. Judson
Decision Analytics
1500 Fort Trail
Accokeek MD 20607
USA
e-mail: DHJudson@comcast.net

Prof. David A. Swanson
Department of Sociology
University of California
1223 Watkins Hall, Riverside
CA 92521
USA
e-mail: dswanson@ucr.edu

ISSN 2211-3215
e-ISSN 2211-3223

ISBN 978-94-007-1271-3
e-ISBN 978-94-007-1272-0

DOI 10.1007/978-94-007-1272-0

Springer Dordrecht Heidelberg London New York

© David A. Swanson 2011

No part of this work may be reproduced, stored in a retrieval system, or transmitted in any form or by any means, electronic, mechanical, photocopying, microfilming, recording or otherwise, without written permission from the Publisher, with the exception of any material supplied specifically for the purpose of being entered and executed on a computer system, for exclusive use by the purchaser of the work.

Cover design: eStudio Calamar, Berlin/Figueres

Printed on acid-free paper

Springer is part of Springer Science+Business Media (www.springer.com)

Contents

Estimating Characteristics of the Foreign Born by Legal Status: An Evaluation of Data and Methods

Abstract This paper starts with a general background regarding issues associated with measuring the foreign born and immigration before describing population estimation techniques. It then describes methods for estimating the foreign-born, including residual methods, administrative records methods, specialized survey methods, and methods that do not fit neatly into the preceding categories. Following the evaluations of these methods are suggestions in regard to data and methods, that could be used to generate regular estimates of the foreign-born by legal status. The paper notes that there is no gold standard for evaluating methods for estimating the foreign-born, which means they cannot be subjected to the standard evaluation process used for the general methods of population estimation. Thus, the selection of methods is based on criteria other than accuracy. These include cost and timeliness, and transparency, among others. The paper concludes with a general recommendation that a "direct" measure of the foreign-born population be developed, and discusses three possibilities: (1) a large scale "two-card" survey be funded and implemented by a non-governmental entity that has the experience and human capital to implement such a survey, (2) an attempt to use existing data sources to cluster or perform a latent class analysis to assign legal status, and (3) an imputation model based on a survey that asks a question on legal status.

Keywords Immigration · Foreign Born Population · Estimation Methods · Legal Status

Introduction

This paper is intended to provide demographers and statisticians with an overview and thorough literature review of methods for estimating characteristics of the foreign-born population by legal status. The key phrase in the above sentence is

D. H. Judson and D. A. Swanson, *Estimating Characteristics of the Foreign Born by Legal Status*, SpringerBriefs in Population Studies, 2,
DOI: 10.1007/978-94-007-1272-0_1, © David A. Swanson 2011

"legal status"; the term itself is difficult to define clearly (although we will make an attempt), and existing surveys and the Decennial Census omit questions referring to legal status, with the exception of naturalization status. In the absence of direct data collection, social scientists must rely on "indirect" methods, which we will describe. Likewise we will discuss data availability and data gaps, and administrative arrangements that might help close the gaps. We will focus only on the national level; while subnational characteristics estimates by legal status would be desirable, at this point such an effort would be "putting the cart before the horse." At points we will simply refer to "status"; in these cases we mean "legal status."

The substantive remainder of the paper is organized into eight sections. The following section provides a general background to issues associated with measuring the foreign born and immigration. It is not meant to be inclusive, but suggestive. The third section deals with population estimation as a whole and includes topics related to direct and indirect measures, formal demography, censuses, and samples. The fourth section deals with estimating the foreign born using residual methods, which are based on the Decennial Census, the Current Population Survey, and, more recently, the American Community Survey. The fifth section deals with estimating the foreign born using administrative records while the sixth section covers method for estimating the foreign born using specialized survey and related statistical methods. The seventh section provides an evaluation of the methods used to estimate the foreign born. The eighth and final section provides suggestions in regard to data and methods that could be used to generate regular estimates of the foreign born by status.

The Foreign Born and Immigration[1]

Overview

As Gerstle (2008) has observed, the history of the United States is deeply intertwined with immigration and for most of its history the country has been remarkably open to immigrants. In fact, it is this immigration that has largely determined the history of the racial and ethnic composition of the United States and its majority–minority relations. Territorial expansion, the incorporation of the people living within these acquired territories, and the "great migration" of African-Americans out of the south, round out the story of the nation's racial and ethnic composition and majority–minority relations (Flanagan 2002).

With the exception of the 1860s and the 1890s, the number of international migrants to the United States increased in each decade from the 1820s to the 1901–1910 decade (Schmidley 2001). The Decennial Census data show that the

[1] Material in this section is adapted from several sources, including Deardorff and Blumerman (2001), Edmonston and Michalowski (2004), Judson (2006), and Malone et al. (2003).

foreign-born population increased rapidly from 2.2 million in 1850, the first year in which place-of-birth data were collected, to 13.5 million in 1910 (Schmidley 2001).

The number of new foreign born arrivals declined between 1911 and the 1920s, due first to World War I and then to the restrictive immigration legislation enacted in 1921 and 1924 in which a national origin quota system was established. This system severely limited immigration and favored countries in the Western Hemisphere and Northern or Western Europe (Schmidley 2001). Because of decreased migration to the United States, the proportion of foreign-born in the total population, which had fluctuated in the 13–15% range from 1860 to 1920, dropped from 14.7% in 1910 to 11.6% in 1930. By 1950, the U.S. foreign-born population dropped to 10.3 million in 1950 or 6.9% of the total population. By 1970 it was down to about 9.8 million, which, at about 4.8% of the total population, represented a record low in the twentieth century (Hansen and Bachu 1995).

Given the often tumultuous nature of racial and ethnic relations in the United States, it comes as no surprise that Americans have also feared immigrants and responses—both physical and legal—have been aimed at specific groups who were viewed as threatening (Gerstle 2008). A landmark response came in the form of the national origins quota system, which was enacted in the 1920s and reaffirmed in the Immigration and Nationality Act of 1952. However, attitudes shifted by the 1960s and the national origins quota was eliminated by the 1965 Amendments to the Immigration and Nationality Act of 1952 (Schmidley 2001). This legislation and subsequent legislation, including the Immigration Reform and Control Act of 1986, which permitted some illegal aliens to obtain lawful permanent residence, and the Immigration Act of 1990, which increased the annual cap on immigration, have contributed to increased international migration (Schmidley 2001).

Since 1970, the numbers of foreign-born have increased, reaching 31.1 million, or 11.1% of the U.S. population, by 2000 (Malone et al. 2003). By 2003, the U.S. Census Bureau estimated the foreign-born population at 33.5 million (Larsen 2004), or approximately 11.5% of the total U.S. population.

While there are uncertainties in the counts and estimates of the foreign-born population, they appear to be less than those for estimates of the foreign-born who are not "authorized" to reside in the United States. Walsh (2007), for example, reports seeing estimates ranging from 7 million to 20 million—even 40 million in one extreme case. However, when in examining estimates that provide descriptions of the methods and data underlying them, the range of numbers is reduced considerably. Passel et al. (2004) estimate that there were 8.3 million unauthorized people residing in the US in 2000. Passel (2005) estimates that there were 10.3 million in 2004. Hoefer et al. (2007) estimate that there were 11.6 as of January 2006, while Fortuny et al. (2007), for example, estimate that in 2007 there were between 11 and 12 million. If the current number is between 11 and 12 million, it would represent about one-third of the foreign-born population in the US.

Just as the uncertainty increases in moving from estimates of the foreign-born population to estimates of the unauthorized population, so does the level of contentiousness. Gerstle (2008), for example, points out that the historical record shows that war or near-war conditions often are associated with less-than enthusiastic "responses" to immigrants. Given the current situation of the United States with troops in Iraq and Afghanistan, it again should come as no surprise that historical tensions have once again arisen between those who "were already here" and those who "have recently arrived."

One example of the contentiousness can be found in a recent paper by Walsh (2007, p. 220), who refers to a 2005 report done by Passel as "…largely advo-babble (immigrant advocate babble) under the guise of research and statistical analysis…" Others view this same report as valid research (see, e.g., National Research Council 2006b; Orrenius and Zavodny 2006; State of Minnesota 2005). We point out the contentiousness surrounding this issue because it affects not only the estimates and other determinations of the foreign-born in the United States, especially when status (i.e., authorized and unauthorized) is considered, but also the task of evaluating the methods used to determine the numbers of foreign-born (Walashek and Swanson 2006). The present "climate" noted, the present paper is aimed at identifying, describing, and evaluating methods that have, are, or could be used to estimate the US foreign-born population by status.

Counting the Foreign Born

Attempts to count the foreign-born population in the United States have a long history. They appear to have started with the 1820 and 1830 decennial censuses, in which enumerators were asked to take note of individuals who were aliens (see, e.g., Malone et al. 2003). However, no specific questions on citizenship status were asked until the 1890 census. These questions remained with some variations except in 1960. Questions concerning an individual's place of birth have appeared in the decennial censuses since 1850.

From 1870 to 1970, parental nativity (place of birth of the individual's father and mother) was also asked. Census 2000 asked, "Where was this person born?" asking for the name of the state for those born within the United States or the country name for those born elsewhere. In many decennial censuses, an additional question asked the year in which a person born outside the United States (whether native or foreign born) came to live in the United States. However, as noted by Grieco (2003) because there is no "long form" planned for the 2010 census, these questions are now found within the American Community Survey (ACS). Unfortunately, as is discussed later, the ACS uses a different definition of residency than does the decennial census, one that is essentially that for a De facto population rather than the De jure definition used in the Decennial Census, the CPS, SIPP, and the Census Bureau's estimates and projections programs (see, e.g., National Research Council 2007, p. 31, 2006a). This is a point to which we return several times.

Currently, the ACS (2008 Questionnaire) asks three questions in regard to the foreign born. These questions are similar to those just described for the decennial censuses. For example, there is an ACS question that asks if one was born in the United States or out of the United States.

Definitions of Foreign Born and Immigrants by "Status"

The U.S. Census Bureau defines the foreign born as people who are not U.S. citizens at birth (Deardorff and Blumerman 2001). This population consists of legal immigrants, temporary migrants, and unauthorized migrants as shown in the following equation (Deardorff and Blumerman 2001):

$$\mathrm{FB} = [L - (M + E) + T + R],$$

where,

FB Foreign-born population;
L Legal Immigrants;
M Mortality to legal immigrants;
E Emigration of legal immigrants;
T Temporary (legal) migrants; and
R Residual foreign-born (unauthorized and quasi-legal migrants).

The preceding equation is a useful way to look at the foreign-born as a whole as well as by status. Among other reasons, it serves as an illustration of the "residual" method for estimating the unauthorized and quasi-legal migrants, a topic that is covered later.

Although the definitions by Deardorff and Blumerman (2001) are useful, there is no single set of conventions used to describe the "status" categories that immigrants fall into (see, e.g., Edmonston and Michalowski 2004; Passel et al. 2004). One of the major sources of confusion in terms of defining immigration status categories involves foreign-born residents with applications pending. Some of these pending applications have different objectives and potential immigration status outcomes. In other cases, an immigration status may be determined in order develop estimates of immigrants by status category. As three simple examples of the former, immigrants may petition to become lawful legal permanent residents, receive changes in temporary or non-immigrant status, or to obtain extensions of non-immigrant status. In terms of the latter, valid reasons exist for interpreting the immigration status of the resident foreign-born population in multiple ways. As two simple examples, an agency may need to render a legal classification for enforcement, budget, or program purposes, while a policymaker may want an estimate of how many foreign-born residents may be affected by proposed legislation. These simple examples point toward the fact that there is neither a single data set nor a single method that can be used to estimate numbers of foreign-born residents with pending applications by immigration status.

There also are two additional situations that may in fact be combined in some situations. First, some of them have "employment authorization documents"; and second, some of them are not legally entitled to be in the United States. In combination, then, some of the foreign-born with employment authorization documents may not be legally entitled to be in the United States.

Further complicating these definitions is the issue of the residence rule used, De jure or De facto. If data from the Decennial Census, CPS, and SIPP are used to generate estimates of the foreign-born by status, then the result is the De jure foreign-born population (by status); if the ACS is used, the result is, in essence, the De facto foreign-born population (by status). As is discussed later, it is not clear what results when DHS data and some other types of administrative data are used. The situation with special surveys aimed at directly counting the foreign-born (by status) also has some ambiguity: a given survey could be aimed at either the De jure or De facto population.

These situations and statuses interact, thereby contributing to the lack of standard definitions and conventions on how to define the foreign-born with pending applications. Are they legal? Are they unauthorized? The Department of Homeland Security (DHS), for example, uses the term "unauthorized" to describe foreign-born persons residing illegally in the United States, but includes some "unauthorized immigrants" who have pending applications.

Given the lack of consensus, Judson (2006) constructed a table that attempts to bring some order to this situation. It is reproduced here as Exhibit 1 and forms a

Exhibit 1 Legal status terms

Term	Sub-term	Legal and procedural definition
(Authorized) Legal immigrant		
	Naturalized	Has obtained U.S. citizenship
	Lawful permanent resident (LPR)	Has applied for LPR status, and has been formally admitted
(Authorized) Legal temporary ("legal non-immigrant")		Lawful temporary application has been accepted; AND
		Terms of admission have not been violated; AND
		Neither naturalized nor LPR status has been granted, even if application exists
Refugee/asylee		Has applied for refugee or asylee status and been granted same; OR
		Present in the U.S., citizen of temporary protected status-recognized country; AND
		Has not converted status to legal temporary, lawful permanent, or naturalized
Residual, unauthorized* or other		Application in process but not yet granted; OR
		Entered without inspection; OR
		Violated terms of residence
	Within residual:	
	Quasi-legal	Has applied for lawful permanent resident, legal temporary status, refugee, asylee, or temporary protected status; AND status not yet granted

useful point of departure for this report in terms of discussing the various categories into which the foreign-born whose place of residence is in the United States as of July 1st (the official estimate date) or April 1st (the official census day) might be classified.

With the exception of the methods based solely on the ACS, most of the different ways that the authors covered in this section have the defined the foreign-born population (by status) are based on the De jure concept of a population, which is the definition used to enumerate the population in the decennial census of the United States. However, this is not always explicit, which is not surprising because the major sources of population data in the United States also are based on this approach (see, e.g., National Research Council 2006a). However, there may be a significant proportion of the unauthorized population that would not be considered as "residents" according to the census enumeration procedures used by the US Census Bureau. Consequently, instead of being enumerated as part of the De jure population, those who do not meet the "residence rules" requirements would not be enumerated because they would be considered as part of the De facto population. In later sections, the effect of these implied definitions on estimates is discussed, especially in terms of estimates generated by the residual method and its variations. Unless otherwise specified, we generally use the term "unauthorized" in this report to described those who would be enumerated in a census as a resident of a given location, but, in fact, entered the United States without inspection, or have an application in process that has not yet been granted, or have violated terms of "legal residence" in the United States.

Current Sources of Data on Immigrants

Edmonston and Michalowski (2004) observe that official records of immigration to the United States have been kept by a Federal agency since 1820, but official records of emigration have been kept only since 1908. The Department of State, the Department of Labor, and other Departments compiled the statistics before this work was shifted from the Department of Labor to the Justice Department in 1944, where it is now located (Edmonston and Michalowski 2004).

The data on migration of the Immigration and Naturalization Service do not fit any simple classification scheme and, in fact, because of the complexity and variety of the data, more than one classification scheme is required to present them (see, e.g., Camarota and Capizzano 2004). Edmonston and Michalowski (2004) identify two principal collection systems and a few subsidiary and supplementary ones. The first is confined to aliens and is based on visa forms surrendered by aliens at ports of entry and visas issued to aliens adjusting their status in the country to permanent residence. This system is believed to cover only a small part of the movement across the United States borders (e.g., Camarota and Capizzano 2004).

The second principal collection system is more inclusive than the first and, in general, covers all persons arriving at and departing from U.S. ports of entry. From a demographic point of view, however, these data have serious limitations not shared by the first classification, including lack of the more detailed information collected. This system covers three subsidiary groups: passengers arriving or departing principally by sea or air, land border crossers, and crewmen. The types of statistics compiled and their precise definitions vary from one period to another. The description given below (Edmonston and Michalowski 2004) applies to the current situation.

> In general, "admission statistics" covers four classes: (1) aliens admitted to the United States as "immigrant aliens admitted," (2) aliens departing from the United States as "emigrant aliens departed," (3) aliens admitted as "non-immigrant aliens admitted," and (4) aliens departing as "non-emigrant aliens departed." Immigrant aliens are nonresident aliens admitted to the United States for permanent residence (or with the declared intention of residing here permanently) or persons residing in the United States as non-immigrants, refugees, or "parolees" who acquired permanent residence through adjustment of their status.
>
> Emigrant aliens are resident aliens departing from the United States for a permanent residence abroad (or with the declared intention of residing permanently abroad). Statistics on emigrant aliens were discontinued as of July 1, 1957, when persons departing were no longer inspected.
>
> The first two classes, which are considered as the basic classes of alien migrants, are supplemented by two additional classes of alien admissions or departures—non-immigrant aliens admitted and non-emigrant aliens departed. In general, non-immigrant aliens are non-resident aliens admitted to the United States for a temporary period or resident aliens returning to an established residence in the United States after a temporary stay abroad (i.e., an absence of more than 12 months). On the basis of recent experience, numerically the most important group of non-immigrant aliens is the group "temporary visitors for pleasure." Other numerically important groups are "returning residents," "temporary visitors for business," "transit aliens," "temporary workers and industrial trainees," and "students." Also included among non-immigrant aliens are "foreign government officials," "exchange aliens," and members of international organizations.
>
> "Non-emigrant aliens departed" are nonresident aliens departing after a temporary stay in the United States or resident aliens departing for a temporary stay abroad (i.e., for more than 12 months). Data on non-emigrant aliens were tabulated up to July 1, 1956; such figures are not available since that date. The classes of arrival and the classes of departure do not correspond to each other completely because the intended length of stay as declared does not always correspond to the actual length of stay. Thus, persons who are admitted as non-immigrant aliens for a temporary stay but remain longer than a year are classified as emigrant aliens on departure, and aliens who are admitted for permanent residence but decide to depart within a year are classified as non-emigrant aliens on departure.
>
> The second collection system provides "arrival" and "departure" statistics and may be viewed as having three distinct components. The first component covers principally arrivals and departures by sea and air; the second covers "border crossers," i.e., persons who cross frequently to or from Canada or Mexico; and the third covers crewmen. The statistics are classified by citizenship. The first component may also be designated as "passenger" statistics: the count is derived from lists of names on passenger manifests prepared by thc airlines and steamship companies.
>
> The second component, "border crossers," represents principally a count, made by immigration inspectors at established points of entry, of persons entering the United States over its land borders with Canada and Mexico. It is a count of crossings; hence, the same persons may be counted more than once. As mentioned above, in addition to the two basic classes of international migrants (immigrants or "new permanent arrivals" and emigrants

departing or "permanent resident departures"), some statistical information is secured for several other groups of persons who cross the borders of the United States. Some account should be taken of these other groups in any assessment of the impact of immigration on the population, particularly on the De facto population: Particular attention should be given to:

1. Non-immigrants. Most non-immigrants are tourists whose visits range from a few days to a few months. A large number of other non-immigrants are business people who stay typically for less than a few weeks. Non-immigrants, however, also include several groups who usually stay in the United States for several months or more. Among them are government officials, students, and temporary workers as well as their spouses and children. In recent years, about one million non-immigrants enter the United States annually for longer periods of residence.

2. Aliens paroled into the United States. From time to time, special legislation allows political refugees to enter and remain in the United States outside the requirements of the Immigration Act. Refugees from Hungary after the revolution in 1956, refugees from the Communist regime in Cuba in the 1960s, and El Salvadorians in the 1990s were granted asylum by special legislation.

3. Arrivals from and departures to the outlying areas of the United States. In the basic tabulations on admissions, the United States and its outlying areas are treated as a unit. Data on movement between the United States and Puerto Rico are currently available, however, in the form of passenger statistics compiled by Puerto Rican authorities.

4. U.S. military personnel. Direct data are not available but their number may be estimated from data on the number of U.S. military personnel overseas given in census reports and reports of the U.S. Department of Defense.

5. Illegal entrants and unrecorded departures.

6. Aliens deported from the United States or departing voluntarily under deportation proceedings. During 1997, 1,537,000 deportable aliens were located. Almost all deportees had entered the United States without inspection and were removed under conditions of voluntary departure.

7. Except daily commuting, all of the movement across a country's borders, however temporary, should be considered demographically significant in relation to a De facto count of the population. The groups of migrants who would be considered consistent with a De jure count of the population would be much more restricted. In the case of the United States, these include members of the armed forces who are transferred into and out of the United States; all "immigrant aliens admitted" and "emigrant aliens departed;" certain classes of "non-immigrant aliens admitted" and "non-emigrant aliens departed" (such as students, resident aliens arriving and departing, some temporary visitors for business, and temporary workers and industrial trainees); "refugees" and "parolees" who enter under special legislation and may later have their status adjusted to that of permanent residence; and citizens who change their usual residence (movement to or from outlying areas and foreign countries). The discontinuance of data collection for certain of these categories (emigrant and non-emigrant aliens departed) and the volatility of the figures for passenger movement (citizens arrived and departed, aliens departed) present a challenge in estimation of additions through immigration to the De jure population."

Edmonston and Michalowski (2004) note that the quality of data on international migration based on frontier control operations is generally much poorer than that of census counts or birth and death statistics. Such data tend to suffer from serious problems of completeness and international comparability. They go on to note that there are several reasons for the poor quality of the data. First, there are many forms of international movement, and they are not easy to define or classify. Second, classification based on duration of stay or purpose of migration depends on statements of intentions, and the actual movements may not correspond to these statements of intentions. Next, the mere counting of persons on the move is extremely difficult, especially when a country has a very long boundary that is poorly patrolled. It is certain that many international migrants enter or leave a country unrecorded under these conditions. Controls over departures are usually less strict than over arrivals so that statistics of emigration are more difficult to collect and less accurate than statistics of immigration. Given these shortcomings, it is not surprising that the United Nations considers that, where available, population register data are the most satisfactory for the measurement of international migration (Edmonston and Michalowski 2004).

As can be deduced partially from the preceding discussion on immigration and emigration, there are neither federal administrative records nor federal survey data sources that directly provide information on the foreign born in the United States who lack documents demonstrating that they are legally in the U.S., whether as members of the De jure population or as part of the De facto population. However, there are three federal agencies that currently collect information on the foreign born: (1) the Census Bureau; (2) the Department of Homeland Security; and (3) The National Center for Health Statistics. The Census Bureau collects this information via two major vehicles: (1) the decennial census; and (2) the American Community Survey (ACS). Other vehicles include the Survey of Income and Program Participation (SIPP) and the Current Population Survey (CPS), in its annual (March) social and economic supplement. The decennial census, SIPP, and the CPS are aimed at the De jure population, while the ACS is aimed at the De facto population.

The Department of Homeland Security's Office of Immigration Statistics (OIS) collects information on the foreign-born via several administrative records systems. One is the Non-Immigrant Information System (NIIS). Another is comprised of records maintained by the U.S. Citizenship and Immigration Services (USCIS). It is not clear if the NIIS is aimed at the De jure population, the De facto population, or a combination of both. The USCIS appears to be aimed at the De jure population. Both OIS and USCIS were part of the former Immigration and Naturalization Service (INS).

The National Center for Health Statistics collects place-of-birth information that is found on death certificates. However, death certificates collect neither information on citizenship nor on status for the foreign born. Certificates do show, however, place of occurrence for each death and place of residence of each decedent. Thus, the death certificates could be used in conjunction with methods aimed at estimating either the De jure or De facto population. Birth certificates have similar information.

Similar to the federal government, no state governments collect information that directly provides information on the foreign born who lack documents of legal residence. However, there are data collections, none of which is either routine or broadly-based, that have been done by individual researchers (see, e.g., Droitcour and Larson 2002; Golden 2008; Heer 1979; Heer and Passel 1987; Marcelli and Heer 1998; North and Houston 1976).

Coupled with the lack of data on the foreign born, particularly in terms of legal status, is an intense interest on the part of policy makers and others on the foreign born, particularly their legal status. A current example of this intense interest is the exclusion of unauthorized persons and some lawful permanent residents from state health exchanges, and other mandates, in the recent health care reform law (Capps et al. 2009; Martin and Burke 2010). Not surprisingly, there is a demand for data on the part of those who are intensely interested and with the lack of data from census, survey, and administrative activities, estimation methods have been used to fill the information gap.

General Methods of Population Estimation[2]

The most complete and reliable source of information on the U.S. population is taken from a census. (Other countries, of course, use administrative records and other sources.) In the United States (and in Canada), the census is based on the concept of a De jure population while in Mexico it is based on the concept of a De facto population (Thorvaldsen 2006). However, a complete enumeration of a population is costly and not all populations have been subject to a census. Even in countries such as the United States, where census counts have been mandated since 1790, their high costs only allow them to be done once every ten years. This means that data can become outdated and that a substitute is needed—a set of population estimates. The development of methods of population estimation roughly corresponds to the development of censuses and vital statistics registries. For example, in the late seventeenth century, John Graunt estimated the population of London and then of the whole of England and Wales using what today we would call a censal-ratio method (Devlin 2008, pp. 93–94). Not long afterward, in the eighteenth century, the French mathematician, Laplace, also used a censal-ratio method in combination with recorded births and a population sample to estimate the population of France (Stigler 1986, pp. 163–164). However, methodological development really only took off in the late 1930s and early 1940s, fueled in large part by the need for low-cost and timely information generated by the great depression of the 1930s and World War II (Bryan 2004; Eldridge 1947; Hauser and Tepping 1944; Shryock 1938; Shryock and Lawrence 1949). In the United States, the Census Bureau played a major role in this effort, but it was not alone. During the early 1940s, the Washington State Census Board, for example, developed a comprehensive program of annual population determinations based on estimation methods that are still used today (Swanson and Pol 2005, 2008). Around this same time, demographers also began developing estimation methods for what were then called "underdeveloped countries," (Brass 1968;

[2] Material in this section is adapted from Swanson and Pol (2005).

Chandrasekaran and Deming 1949; Popoff and Judson 2004; United Nations 1969) and the use of sample surveys as a substitute for complete census counts took hold (Bryan 2004).

Today, population estimates are ubiquitous. They are done around the world by a host of governmental and non-governmental entities, as well as individual consultants (Bryan 2004; Siegel 2002; Swanson and Pol 2008). The widespread availability of data, methods, and technology has made is possible for many people not only to develop estimates, but to do so more quickly and less expensively than has ever been done before. This trend is not likely to abate, but it carries with it a cost in that estimates may both be made and used with little or no understanding of the issues involved, what constitutes "good" estimates, and how to identify them (see, e.g., Judson 2007).

What is a Population Estimate?

A population estimate is the determination of the size or the characteristics of a population at a current or past date in the absence of census data for the same date. In the United Sates, they usually are made on a De jure basis, which makes sense because it is the De jure population that is desired in the United States and such an estimate generally makes use of historical census data. However, there is a need for De facto estimates on occasion (e.g., for "daytime population") and researchers have developed these estimates (Swanson and Pol 2005, 2008). Also, as noted earlier, the ACS represents a major break with this history in that it effectively is targeted at the De facto, rather than the De jure population (National Research Council 2006a). While the American Community Survey effectively counts a De facto population, it is important to note that the raw numbers are then controlled to a De jure population (National Research Council 2007; Swanson and Hough 2007).

The term "population estimate" is frequently used in the public domain to refer to the determination of the size or the characteristics of a population at a future date. However, most demographers prefer to use the term projection when talking about the possible size and characteristics of a population in the future. In developing a portrait of a given population in the future, it is not uncommon for a series of projections to be made that incorporate a range of plausible assumptions (e.g., expected trends in fertility, mortality, and migration). However, when one of these projections is selected as representing the most likely future, it then becomes the forecast for the population in question.

As opposed to a projection or a forecast, then, a population estimate is concerned with either the present or the past, but not the future (Smith et al. 2001, pp. 3–4). Typically, the purpose of an estimate is to construct what a census *would have enumerated*, if such a census had taken place on the estimate date.

An estimate can be prepared for a nation or a sub-national area such as a state, county, city, town, or census tract. An estimate also can be prepared for groups of sub-national areas, groups of nations, or even the world as a whole. The principal demographic characteristics for which an estimate is made include age and gender. However, in multiracial and multi-ethnic countries such as the United States, Canada, and the United Kingdom, an estimate might be constructed not only by age and gender, but also by race and ethnicity. An estimate also can be made of social and economic sub-groups of the population, households, and families.

Types of Estimation Methods

Demographers and statisticians have developed a population estimation toolkit that contains a range of methods designed to meet different information needs at varying levels of accuracy and cost. For the most part they are based on the concept of a De jure population although there are exceptions (Swanson and Pol 2005). The methods can be roughly placed into three categories: (1) analytical and statistical models that use data symptomatic of population and its changes; (2) mathematical models that use historical census data; and (3) sample surveys. Methods falling into the first category have generally been developed by and for applied demographers, most of whom work for national, state, and local governments. Methods falling into the second category have generally developed by and for academic demographers, most of whom work at universities and research institutes. The methods falling into the third category have generally been developed by and for statisticians and survey research scientists, but they also are widely used by demographers. Not surprisingly, there also are techniques that combine methods from two or even all three categories.

It also is useful to classify population estimates along a temporal dimension: (1) intercensal estimates, which refer to a date between two census counts and usually take the results of both counts into consideration; (2) postcensal estimates, which refer to a date subsequent to the latest census count and usually into account one or more previous census counts; and (3) pre-censal estimates, which refer to a date prior to a census count, but usually take into account one or more subsequent census counts. This temporal classification is useful because different methods are typically employed in the development of intercensal, postcensal, and pre-censal estimates (Bryan 2004).

There are other schema for classifying estimation methods. Long (1993), for example, categorizes them generally into two types: (1) "flow" methods; and (2) "stock" methods. Flow methods are also known as component methods, because they require estimation of each component of population change since the last census. Stock methods relate changes in population size since the last census to changes in other measured variables: the number of housing units, automobile registrations, total number of deaths (and births), and tax returns. Long also notes that stock and flow methods may be used in combination, as is the case with some of the methods we describe later.

Estimating the Foreign Born by Legal Status

In addition to the schema described in general for population estimation, methods for estimating the foreign-born can be classified along other lines. Judson (2006) in evaluating four methods of estimating the foreign-born, for example, classifies them into three groups. The first he calls a "stock estimate using a residual component" (Passel et al. 2004; Cassidy 2004a, b). He labels the second group "flow-based stock estimates (Judson 2006) and the third, "an imputation modeling method" (Judson 2006).

In this report, a variation of Judson's classification scheme is used, one which has four primary categories. The first is comprised of "residual methods," which are based on Census Bureau products such as the Decennial Census, the Current Population Survey, and, more recently, the American Community Survey. There is some ambiguity here in that the Decennial Census and the Current Population Survey are both based on the concept of a De jure population, while the ACS is effectively based on the concept of the De facto population (National Research Council 2006a). The second is made up of "administrative records methods," which are based on records collected and maintained by, for example, the Department of Homeland Security. It is not clear if these data are based on a De jure or De facto concept. The third is "specialized direct methods," which, as the name suggests, are designed to obtain direct (rather than residual) status information on the foreign-born. These methods can be targeted at either a De jure or De facto population (or both simultaneously).

The fourth and final category consists of methods not otherwise described and includes, for example, the "sex-ratio" method (Bean et al. 1983). Since this method uses vital statistics data from the United States in conjunction with census data from the United States and Mexico, it inherently represents a combination of the De jure and De facto concepts. Both the "Death Registration" and the "Birth Registration" methods described by GAO (1993) are essentially based on the De jure concept, although either one could be a mixture of both if deaths and births by place of occurrence are used in conjunction with the vital rates method (Bogue 1950) instead of deaths and births by place of residence.

As was noted by Long (1993) in regard to stock and flow methods, the methods in the classification system used here can be combined. Thus, these four primary categories are sub-divided into stock and flow methods, or combinations of stock and flow methods, as appropriate. Finally, it is useful to note here that any system for classifying methods of population estimation (or methods of population projection, for that matter) is inconsistent in that none is mutually exclusive and exhaustive.

Estimating the Foreign Born Using Residual Methods[3]

The use of the a residual estimate for estimating the foreign born is primarily, but not exclusively, aimed at estimating those who lack legal documents (see, e.g., Deardorff and Blumerman 2001; Passel et al. 2004; Van Hook and Bean 1998). There are several variations of the "residual" method for this purpose. Many of them are members of the "stock method" in that they attempt to estimate the number without legal documents as the difference between the non-citizen population enumerated in a census or a survey (i.e., the Current Population Survey or the American Community Survey) and the legally resident alien population, where enumerated unauthorized resident migrants = enumerated non-citizens − legally resident aliens. Others are "flow-based" residual methods.

In general, the residual methods can be done by national origin, period of entry, age, sex, and depending on the level of detail available in estimates of the legal population, by state and metropolitan area.

"Stock-Based" Residual Methods

GAO (1993, p. 21) provides a general form of the stock-based residual method as follows:

$$I = F - L,$$

where,

- I Estimated illegal alien population;
- F The counted foreign-born population; and
- L An independent estimate of the total legally resident foreign-born population.

GAO (1993, p. 21) notes that "L" in their analysis was constructed on the basis of the latest available (1980) data obtained from the Alien Registration Program, to which were added estimated legal immigration from permanent INS files and to which were subtracted the estimated emigration of foreign-born persons.

The Passel, Van Hook, and Bean Residual Method of 2004

In this "stock-based" residual method, Passel et al. (2004) attempted to match micro-data from the Decennial long form and the ACS (e.g., a person's place of

[3] Material in this section is adapted from several sources, including Deardorff and Blumerman (2001), Judson (2006), and Passel et al. (2004).

birth, year of entry, age, sex, education, occupation, and spousal characteristics) to the requirements for the legal statuses: naturalized citizens, non-immigrants, and refugees/asylees. Each of the foreign-born observations in the micro-dataset is attempted to be assigned to one of these three statuses. All cases that do not match the criteria of one of the legal statuses are considered to be in the residual category, which includes both the unauthorized (e.g. entries without inspection and visa over-stayers) and the quasi-legal. The estimate of the residual category of the foreign born is then calculated as either: (1) the total weighted number of people in the residual category; or (2) the total foreign born population subtracting the weighted estimates of naturalized citizens, lawful permanent residents, and legal non-immigrants.

Because this method uses survey data, all of the limitations of survey data apply (e.g., measurement error, non-response error, coverage error, and sample error). In addition, this method not only assumes that the assignment algorithm accurately measures legal status, but it also assigns respondents with the same characteristics into the same legal status. This means that the components are constructed from imputations of legal status rather than from known legal status, which in turn means that some cases with characteristics that appear to match the criteria of a legal category may not actually have that legal status, while others who, by their surveyed characteristics, appear not to match a legal category may still have that legal status.

In spite of these limitations, the method due to Passel et al. (2004) has several strengths. First, it is flexible and can be adapted to future changes in definitions of legal status. Second, the algorithms can be reproduced under alternate assumptions regarding the matching between the micro-data information and visa or LPR criteria. Third, this method can potentially be used with data sets that have information similar to that found in the 2000 Decennial Long form and the ACS. If used with the former (or the CPS), it targets the De jure foreign-born population (by status); if used with the ACS, it targets the De facto foreign-born population (by status); if used with a combination of Decennial Census, ACS, and SIPP on the one hand and the ACS, on the other, the result is a mixture of De jure and De facto populations.

The Residual Method Described by Cassidy in 2004

Another variation of the "stock-based" residual method is found in work by Cassidy (2004a, b). It combines an algorithm for assigning legal temporary migrant status with an algorithm for identifying the probabilities that a migrant has come to the U.S. under voluntary or humanitarian conditions. The method produces estimates of the foreign born population across four distinct legal status categories: (1) Legal Permanent Resident (LPR); (2) Legal Temporary; (3) Quasi-Legal; and (4) Unauthorized. This method starts with the total foreign-born population for a given vintage period of a survey (e.g., Census 2000 long form) and first removes from this pool the naturalized foreign-born. An algorithm then extracts people from the remaining pool who are likely to be LPR's. This extraction includes people who entered the United States more than 10 years prior to the vintage year of the survey, received some form of public assistance, and had children who entered the U.S. prior to them, or whose spouse or householder is a U.S. citizen. The remaining foreign born are subjected to the temporary migrant algorithm, which (put simply) assigns foreign-born people to various legal non-immigrant categories according to various demographic conditions that they meet and performs consistency checks to ensure that spouses and children of assigned legal non-immigrants are also classified as legal non-immigrants. This algorithm operates on 100% assignment based on met criteria. Those people who pass through the temporary migrant algorithm but are not assigned a category represent the residual, which is assumed to contain refugees, asylees, quasi-legal migrants, and unauthorized migrants.

When the four major groups have been formed, the total foreign-born population is then subjected to a "humanitarian status" algorithm. At this stage, each case is assigned the probability of being an involuntary migrant (refugee, asylee, or quasi-legal) on the basis of their country of birth and year of U.S. entry. These probabilities are derived from USCIS administrative records of annual LPR, refugee, and asylee flows. After this process, the probability assigned to each case is multiplied by the person-weight (original or re-weighted) to create a new grouping weight.

When aggregated according to the grouping weight, estimates of humanitarian and voluntary migrants for each migrant status group are generated. Naturalized citizens and legal non-immigrants are not subject to further processing and are left as is. Among the likely LPR's, which represent most of the cases that are assigned to LPR status, the aggregated estimate of voluntary migrants who entered the U.S. between 10 and 20 years before the survey year that do not meet any other condition are assumed to be unauthorized migrants. Finally, among the residual group, the aggregated estimate of involuntary migrants are assumed to be quasi-legal, refugees, or asylees, whereas the aggregated estimate of voluntary migrants are assumed to be unauthorized migrants.

This method shares a number of assumptions, advantages and disadvantages with the method due to Passel et al. (2004) and is aimed at targeting the De jure foreign-born population (by status).

Other "Stock-Based" Residual Methods

Passel (2007) discusses methods of measuring unauthorized migration to the United States. This is a "stock-based" method, which involves comparing an analytic estimate of the legal foreign-born population with a survey-based measure of the total foreign-born population. The difference between the two population figures is a measure of the unauthorized migrant population in the survey; it can then be corrected for omissions to provide a measure of the total unauthorized population. Passel (2007) includes a detailed description of the residual methods and the underlying data and assumptions as it has been applied to recent data from the Current Population Survey (CPS) and decennial censuses. Because this method uses decennial census and CPS data, it is aimed at the De jure foreign-born population (by status).

Passel's (2006) estimate of unauthorized workers is derived by using a variant of a basic "residual" method. That is, the unauthorized population consists of persons and groups not included in the authorized population. To reach that number, the first step is to develop an estimate for the legal, foreign-born population. That estimate is based on admissions into the country provided by the Department of Homeland Security (DHS) and its predecessor, the Immigration and Naturalization Service (INS), as well on the number of refugees admitted and the number of asylum applications granted.

Using data from the March 2004 Current Population Survey, Passel (2005) applies the residual method and estimates that the unauthorized residents reached an estimated 10.3 million in March 2004 with unauthorized Mexicans numbering 5.9 million or 57% of the total. Again, this is aimed at estimating the De jure foreign-born population (by status).

Passel and Woodrow (1984) estimate the number of unauthorized aliens counted in the 1980 census for each state and the District of Columbia using aggregated data derived by a residual technique. This is obviously based on a De jure concept.

Passel and Woodrow (1987) develop estimates of the number of unauthorized aliens included in the April 1983 Current Population Survey (CPS). Their estimates are derived by subtracting an estimate of the legally resident foreign born population from the survey estimate of all foreign born residents. The methodology is similar to that used by Warren and Passel (1987) with the 1980 census and, like it, is aimed at estimating the De jure foreign-born population (by status).

Passel et al. (2004) use data from Census 2000 and other sources, to develop direct estimates of the unauthorized foreign-born population of the United States and six states in the year 2000. The estimates are presented by age, sex, and period of entry for broad country of origin groups and for 29 individual countries of origin. The authors believe that the estimates are the first using Census 2000 data incorporating improved methods for identifying and adjusting directly on the basis of micro-data for the presence of legal non-immigrants (or legal temporary migrants) among the enumerated foreign-born in census data. It is aimed at producing estimates of the De jure foreign-born population (by status).

Van Hook et al. (2006) introduced a new method for estimating foreign-born emigration that takes advantage of the sample design of the Current Population Survey (CPS): repeated interviews of persons in the same housing units over a period of 16 months. Individuals appearing in a first March Supplement to the CPS but not the next include those who died in the intervening year, those who moved within the country, and those who emigrated. They use statistical methods to estimate the proportion of emigrants among those not present in the follow-up interview. They argue that their method produces emigration estimates that are comparable to those from residual methods in the case of longer-term residents (immigrants who arrived more than 10 years ago), but yields higher—and what appear to be more accurate—estimates for recent arrivals. Although somewhat constrained by sample size, they also generate estimates by age, sex, region of birth, and duration of residence in the United States. Because this method is based on the CPS, it is aimed at estimating the De jure foreign-born population (by status).

Warren and Passel (1987) and Passel and Woodrow (1984) use a variation of the residual method to estimate the number of unauthorized aliens counted in the 1980 census for the United States and each state, respectively. The method involves comparison of census figures for aliens counted with estimates of legally-resident aliens developed principally with data from the Immigration and Naturalization Service (INS). For this study, estimates by age, sex, and period of entry were produced for persons born in Mexico and living in Los Angeles County. On the one hand, this is based on the De jure concept because one set of numbers is based on the De jure concept; on the other hand, it is not clear if the INS data are based on the De jure concept, the De facto concept, or a combination of both.

Passel and Woodrow (1987) applied a residual method to data from the April 1983 CPS to estimate of the number of unauthorized foreign-born for the U.S. as a whole. In this case, they subtracted an estimate of the legally resident foreign-born population from the CPS estimate of all foreign born residents. The methodology is similar to that used by Warren and Passel (1987) with the 1980 census. Also presented are similar estimates for the November 1979 CPS, that is, re-estimates following the work of Warren (1982). Estimates are presented by period of entry for Mexico and other groups of countries. Comparison of the April 1983 estimate with the census-based estimate and the November 1979 survey-based estimate provide an indication of growth in the unauthorized alien population for 1980–1983. For this recent period, the implied annual growth in the unauthorized alien population is in the range of 100,000 to 300,000—a range lower than has usually been offered in speculative assessments. The resulting estimate is aimed at the De jure foreign-born population (by status).

Yet another variation of the "Stock-based" residual approach is a "stock" method described by Judson (2006). It can be labeled as the "SIPP Imputation" method. According to Judson (2006), it develops a legal status imputation model from the Survey of Income and Program Participation (SIPP) and applies this model to ACS data, thereby diverging substantially from the preceding three methods. Because it uses both SIPP and ACS data it uses both De jure and De facto population concepts.

Judson (2006) describes this method for using SIPP data as a tool for developing a statistical imputation model as follows:

1. Recode the SIPP questions into categories that can be used to predict legal status using internal Census data, these categories include refugee/asylee, legal permanent resident, and "other");
2. Determine comparability between SIPP and ACS variables and concepts (e.g., age, race and Hispanic origin, and place of birth);
3. Develop a multinomial logistic regression model that uses SIPP data to predict a person's immigration status;

4. Using the estimated parameters from SIPP, apply the model to ACS respondents; and
5. Tabulate ACS respondents by applying predicted probabilities to the ACS person weight thereby creating a vector of probability weights.

Judson (2006) observes that the model that links the two data sets requires equivalent (or approximately equivalent) variables as right hand side predictors. This imputation method is not new; it has been used in place of statistical matching or other hot deck procedures in other contexts (e.g., imputing health insurance status, or imputing tax statuses). As Judson (2006) notes, there are several assumptions underlying this method:

1. The SIPP data can be recoded in a way that is a reasonable representation of the respondent's current migration status;
2. The imputation model will have sufficiently high goodness-of-fit properties to make it feasible to impute individual legal statuses; and
3. The parameters estimated on the SIPP will be successful when applied to ACS.

Judson (2006) also notes that the multinomial logit model in this method allows the use of more refined characteristics to derive estimates, and using a probabilistic approach allows for the creation of probabilistic weights and aggregate estimates by category, and a range of probabilities may be specified for each individual observation, allowing for the extension of micro-simulation. This method allows for multiple estimates, including for sub-groups by age, race, sex, and educational attainment, and is relatively easy to implement. Judson (2006) argues, however, that the main limitation of this method involves the timing and availability of data as follows.

> SIPP estimates are static estimates for spanning January to April 2004. ACS estimates are being derived for multiple years. Policy and behavioral changes that affect immigration patterns may not be captured in the model's vector of probabilities. Another important limitation is that different sample designs are used for data collection. The SIPP sample is a panel where all households are interviewed in a four-month collection window. The ACS sample is collected on a rolling basis using a 12-month reference period corresponding roughly to a calendar year. That along with the fact that we are predicting probabilities based on monthly data while predicting probabilities using annual data is another potential concern. Finally, with a sample size of less than 50,000 households, SIPP's sample is comparatively small relative to other nationally based surveys (e.g., CPS-ASEC and ACS). The foreign-born portion of the SIPP sample is only 9,825 (un-weighted) cases (625 of which are children under the age of 15). These cases form the basis for the imputation model.

"Flow-Based" Variations of the Residual Method

As a concrete example of the "Flow-based" residual method for estimating the unauthorized and quasi-legal migrants, it is useful here to recall the equation due to Deardorff and Blumerman (2001) that was presented earlier:

$$\mathrm{FB} = [L - [M + E] + T + R],$$

where,

FB Foreign-born population;
L Legal Immigrants;
M Mortality to legal immigrants;
E Emigration of legal immigrants;
T Temporary (legal) migrants; and
R Residual foreign-born (unauthorized and quasi-legal migrants).

According to Van Hook and Bean (1998), this method was not employed with data collected prior to 1980 because the 1980 census was the first decennial census in which a sizable enumerated migrant population could be detected through demographic analysis.

Bean et al. (1998) note that while stock and flow estimates of the unauthorized migrant population tended to be unreliable prior to 1980 due in part to lack of methodologies for correcting for biases in the available data sources and otherwise to the fact that these methods tended to be inconsistent in their assumptions and methodologies, that changes that took place in the methods since 1980 and note that these changes have narrowed considerably the range of plausible estimates.

These "flow-based" residual methods include work by Ahmed and Robinson (1994), who attempt to develop estimates of emigration of the foreign-born population at the national level based on the numbers of foreign-born persons enumerated in the 1980 and 1990 censuses. The methodology employed is a residual technique in which the counted population is subtracted from the expected population to obtain the amount of emigration and emigration rates. It is aimed at estimating the De jure foreign-born population (by status).

Bhaskur et al. (2008) employ a residual method to produce contemporary emigration estimates and rates using Census 2000, the 2005 and 2006 American Community Survey (ACS), and National Center for Health Statistics life tables, the latter of which are based on De jure populations. Because this method uses data representing both De jure and De facto population concepts, its results represent a mixture of the two.

Costanzo et al. (2001) evaluate the U.S. Census Bureau's estimates of the "residual" foreign-born population (including both unauthorized and quasi-legal migrants) in 1990 and 2000, in part, by developing a residual-based set of estimates that were calculated in conjunction with estimates of other components of international migration: legal permanent migration and legal temporary migration. The authors note that this residual foreign-born population is not an estimate of the number of unauthorized migrants, but rather, includes people who are here legally but are not yet included in the official estimates of legal migrants and refugees as well as people in "quasi-legal" status who are awaiting action on their legal migration requests. Because the estimate was derived from a residual methodology, any limitations in the methods or in the measurement of other migration components are reflected in the residual number. In addition, their assumptions include a great deal of uncertainty, especially for small migration components. Therefore, the residual they estimate may be quite different from the actual number of unauthorized migrants. According to their calculations, the estimated residual foreign-born population was 3,765,906 in 1990 and 8,705,419 in 2000. The residual foreign born were less likely to be male (48.4%) in 1990 than in 2000 (54.2%). These authors compare De jure estimates produced by the U.S. Census Bureau with numbers produced by the authors that appear to have a mixture of De jure and De facto populations.

Gibbs et al. (2003) examine assumptions about emigration of the native population used by the Census Bureau. From the 1970s through the 1980s, the Census Bureau estimated annual emigration of the native population at a constant level of 27,000. For the 1990–2000 inter-censal decade, the Census Bureau estimated annual emigration of the native population at a constant level of 48,000. The evaluation attempted—unsuccessfully—to replicate the approach taken to arrive at the 48,000 figure. Working with published data from population censuses and statistical reports of other countries, the authors were able to calculate a rough estimate of the net effect of the native emigrant flow on the 2000 national resident population estimate. They compared the available data for dates as close to 1990 and 2000 as possible for 16 countries for which data were available. These 16 countries represented 58% of the American population abroad as measured by 2000 State Department data. They then applied 1990 U.S. survival rates to survive the populations of the 11 countries for which age distribution data were available. The authors note that the limitations on the available data make the estimate of the native emigrant population questionable, but that their research indicates that the magnitude of this population is small and likely to fluctuate over time. Their work is based on a De jure concept, but some of the countries to which U.S. survival rates were applied use the De facto concept in their census enumerations.

Goldberg (1974) uses data on the number of legally admitted aliens and counts of the entire population to estimate the number of illegal aliens. His calculations involve the subtraction of the expected number of people (those who reside legally in the United States) from the actual number of people (those who have been found to be in the United States). Thus, it is basically aimed at the De jure foreign-born population (by status).

Hill (1985) assesses methods to estimate the flows and stock of migrants, and focuses on residual techniques. Hill (1987) presents two methods for estimating migration flows from census data and illustrates them by applications to recent U.S. data. The first method is a simplification of existing intercensal projection methods, and will be affected by changes in census coverage. The second method incorporates independent information on the age pattern of intercensal migration and estimates consistent adjustment factors for census coverage and the scale of the migration schedule. Interpretation of the results of the two methods is discussed. Both of these methods are aimed at estimating the De jure foreign-born population (by status).

Hoefer et al. (2009, 2006, 2007) estimate the number of unauthorized immigrants residing in the United States as of January in a given year by period of entry, region and country of origin, and state of residence. Their estimates were obtained using a "residual" methodology, whereby estimates of the legally resident foreign-born population as of January 1st were subtracted from the total foreign-born population at the same point in time. Estimates of the legally resident foreign-born were based primarily on administrative data of the Department of Homeland Security (DHS), while estimates of the total foreign-born population were obtained from the American Community Survey (ACS) of the U.S. Census Bureau. The starting point for the estimates was 1980, as persons who entered the United States earlier were assumed to be legally resident. Revised estimates of the unauthorized immigrant population living in the United States in 2000 are also presented in this report. These revised estimates are also based on the "residual method" and do not include as legally resident those persons who had applied for but not yet been granted asylum or legal permanent resident (LPR) status as well as Temporary Protected Status (TPS) applicants and beneficiaries. These estimates are based on the De jure concept of population, but in using the ACS, a De jure population is introduced.

Another variation of the residual approach is described by Judson (2006). He labeled it as a "Flow-based, Stock" method because it follows a similar type of demographic accounting procedure to that used for producing national, state and county population estimates for the total resident population. For population estimates, the components of population change are births, deaths, net domestic migration, net international migration and net military movement to and from overseas. However, for estimating foreign-born population by legal status, the appropriate components of population change are more complicated. The equation for each type of legal status category i has the following flow equation between time $t1$ and time $t2$:

$$\mathrm{POP}_{t2} = \mathrm{POP}_{t1} + \mathrm{NA}_{t1}^{t2} + \mathrm{AI}_{t1}^{t2} - \mathrm{AO}_{t1}^{t2} - \mathrm{AE}_{t1}^{t2} - E_{t1}^{t2} - D_{t1}^{t2}$$

where,

POP_{t2} Foreign-born population of legal status i at time $t2$;
POP_{t1} Foreign-born population of legal status i at time $t1$;
NA_{t1}^{t2} New arrival foreign-born population of legal status i between time $t1$ and time $t2$;
AI_{t1}^{t2} Adjustment of foreign-born population into legal status i between time $t1$ and time $t2$;
AO_{t1}^{t2} Adjustment of foreign-born population out of legal status i between time $t1$ and time $t2$;
AE_{t1}^{t2} Foreign-born population of legal status i expelled between time $t1$ and time $t2$;
E_{t1}^{t2} Foreign-born population of legal status i emigrated between time $t1$ and time $t2$; and
D_{t1}^{t2} Foreign-born population of legal status i who died between time $t1$ and time $t2$.

In addition, the sum of each legal status category *i* at time *t* must equal the total estimate of the foreign-born population at time *t*, as shown below.

$$\mathrm{POP}_t^{\mathrm{FB}} = \mathrm{POP}_t^{\mathrm{Nat}} + \mathrm{POP}_t^{\mathrm{LPR}} + \mathrm{POP}_t^{\mathrm{LT}} + \mathrm{POP}_t^{\mathrm{REF}} + \mathrm{POP}_t^{\mathrm{QL}} + \mathrm{POP}_t^{\mathrm{Oth}}$$

where,

FB	Total foreign-born population;
Nat	Naturalized foreign-born population;
LPR	Legal Permanent Resident foreign born population;
LT	Legal Temporary foreign-born population;
REF	Refugee/Asylee foreign born population;
QL	Quasi-legal foreign-born population; and
Oth	Other foreign-born population.

Conceptually, the preceding equation fully represents the appropriate flows of the foreign-born population from one category to another, as well as movement from "outside the system" and exits to "outside the system." Judson (2006) notes, however, that in practice the data sources required to construct a stock estimate based on appropriately accounting for movement between legal status categories have not been available and that a major assumption underlying this approach is that the components of population change are closely approximated by measuring change in selected administrative or survey data sources. Lacking firm numbers on legal temporary flow (in and out), too much inflow is generated by this method and insufficient outflow, which can easily lead to misjudgments about what is too much or too little.

In order to apply the model, Judson (2006) states that Census Bureau demographers estimate each component of population change and legal status category separately. In addition, this method makes the (crucial) assumption that the administrative and survey data that are used to construct demographic flows are comparable; that is, that the time reference, time frame for data production, and concepts can be appropriately compared to one another.

According to Van Hook and Bean (1998), this implementation of the residual method was not employed with data collected prior to 1980 because the 1980 census was the first decennial census in which a sizable enumerated migrant population could be detected through demographic analysis. Van Hook and Bean (1998) identify three variations of this "residual" method.

Bean et al. (1998) note that while stock and flow estimates of the unauthorized migrant population tended to be unreliable prior to 1980 due in part to lack of methodologies for correcting for biases in the available data sources and otherwise to the fact that these methods tended to be inconsistent in their assumptions and methodologies.

This "slippage" between data sources is a significant limitation of this method. Such "slippage" is a result of: (1) Transaction-based data that to-date have not been possible to convert to a person-based estimate; (2) transitions between categories that are as-yet unaccounted for; and (3) the requirement of various assumptions (e.g., foreign-born emigration) deemed to be excessive. As stated in the description of this method, this means that lacking firm numbers on legal temporary flow (in and out), too much inflow is generated by this method and insufficient outflow, which can easily lead to misjudgments about what is too much or too little. Perhaps this could be overcome by conducting a special study on I-94 inflow data such that legal temporary residents could be linked to passenger manifests and I-94 outflow data. Transitions to other statuses might be examined using record linkage methods. The estimates produced by this method appear to be aimed at the De jure population.

Woodrow (1990) discusses the estimation of emigration and unauthorized immigration rates for the United States and uses a residual methodology that compares census or survey data on the resident foreign-born population with an independently derived estimate of the legally resident foreign-born population. The difference is the estimated unauthorized population which may be compared for alternative dates to derive measures of change. Her method is aimed at the De jure population.

Robinson et al. (1993) describe "Demographic Analysis," which is a residual "components of population change" method used as an analytic tool for census coverage measurement. This technique can be used to shed some light, indirect, but illuminating, on the numbers of unauthorized foreign-born around the time of a decennial census. This technique is based on a De jure concept.

Woodrow-Lafield (1995) notes that national surveys monitored growth in the foreign-born population for the 1980s, especially net unauthorized migration's continuing role, but the 1990 census detected an even larger foreign-born population than these surveys. She suggests that under-coverage in 1990 could have been higher than initially presented and observes that assumptions intended to maintain a high net undercount of the unauthorized population performed poorly when census counts of foreign-born residents became known. She argues that any point estimate for net unauthorized migration, calculated as a residual, is likely to be biased by assumptions and data gaps for components of calculating net legal immigration, especially in the direction of underestimation. Despite the importance of unauthorized migration measurement for census evaluation and policy purposes, Woodrow-Lafield (1995) believes that differences among various unauthorized estimates are more likely to stem from discrepancies in universe, reference dates, or individual judgment, rather than analytic refinement. She concludes that better measurement of the foreign born population or its census coverage would aid in setting upper limits on net unauthorized migration. Implied in her analysis, is the fact that she is largely viewing the foreign-born population on a De jure basis.

Estimating the Foreign Born Using Administrative Records

"Administrative Records" have been defined (Judson and Popoff 2004) as "Data collected for an administrative purpose, as opposed to a formal research data collection effort." In our context, such data could be the primary source of information, or a secondary source working in concert with a survey or census. In this section, we will review efforts that "primarily" use administrative records, rather than "secondarily."

Espenshade and Acevedo (1995) examine macro-structural conditions that affect time trends in aggregate probabilities of unauthorized alien apprehension along the Mexico-U.S. border. It shows that the number of migrants attempting to cross the border illegally in a given period and the level of effort expended by the INS to apprehend unauthorized migrants are principal determinants of apprehension probabilities. These findings differ from those by Donato et al. (1992) who argued that individual, household, and community factors are not significant predictors of apprehension probabilities and conclude that escaping INS detection at the border is essentially a random process unrelated to personal traits or to enforcement provisions of the 1986 Immigration Reform and Control Act. Espenshade and Acevedo (1995) conclude that it is worth modeling the effects of individuals' characteristics on apprehension probabilities by including as predictors an estimate of the flow of unauthorized migrants and measures of INS border enforcement effort. The estimates produced by Espenshade and Acevedo are based on data that are De facto in nature while the work of Donato, Duran and Massey, appear to be more inclined toward a De jure perspective, although not exclusively so.

Fernandez (1995) uses the cohort survival method in conjunction with State Department U.S. citizen registration-data to estimate the annual rate of U.S. born emigration. The author claims that the estimates generated, by age, sex, and race are not unreasonable, reaching 48,000 U.S. native born emigrants annually. This appears to be based on a De jure concept.

Grieco (2004) uses a "stock" method based primarily on data from the Department of Homeland Security's Non-immigrant Information System (NIIS). Stock estimates for the total non-immigrant population by category of admission and country of citizenship were generated using this administrative flow data and a "person year" methodology. The results of this analysis suggest that, on a typical day in 2004, there were an estimated 3.8 million non-immigrants in the United States, including 2.3 million tourists, business travelers, and other short-term visitors, 704,000 temporary workers, 640,000 students and exchange visitors, and 68,000 diplomats and other representatives. This method appears to produce a combination of De jure and De facto estimates of the foreign-born population (by status).

Lancaster and Scheuren (1978) speculate on the number of illegal aliens residing in the United States using data from the 1973 CPS-IRS-SSA Exact Match Study, which was conducted by the Census Bureau and the Social Security Administration, assisted by the Internal Revenue Service. Direct estimates are presented only for the age group 18 to 44 years old as of April 1973; however, there are some discussions of ways, using other sources, that one can extend these figures to all age groups and project them forward in time. The estimates produced by Lancaster and Scheuren appear to be largely targeted at a De jure population, but they may include elements of a De facto population

Rytina (2007) presents estimates of the legal permanent resident (LPR) population living in the United States on January 1, 2006. The LPR population includes persons granted lawful permanent residence, e.g. "green card" recipients, but not those who had become U.S. citizens. The estimates are shown for the total LPR population and the LPR population eligible to apply to naturalize by country of birth, state of residence, and the year LPR status was obtained. Data for the estimates were obtained primarily from administrative records of U.S. Citizenship and Immigration Services (USCIS) of the Department of Homeland Security (DHS). The methodology used for the 2006 estimates is similar to that used in previous DHS estimates (see, e.g., Rytina 2004, 2005, 2006). Minor changes in assumptions, made to be consistent with DHS estimates of the unauthorized population, had little effect on the estimates. Rytina's estimate appears to be largely aimed at the De facto population.

U.S. GAO (2004) identified major government sources of data that could be used to estimate illegal alien school children. If used, these data could produce estimates of either the De jure or De facto foreign-born population, or both.

Woodrow-Lafield (1998) focuses on estimating net authorized immigration from all countries and from Mexico and presents 30 alternative series on the basis of varying assumptions as to emigration levels, agricultural legalization beneficiaries as resident, and other nonspecific authorized or ambiguous immigration. Net authorized immigration for 1960–1996 may have resulted in 16.1–19.4 million residents of foreign-born. She argues that measurement is an essential step for quantifying net unauthorized or unauthorized immigration requiring further exercise of expert judgment. Her work appears to be largely aimed at estimating the De jure population of foreign-born.

In our investigation of the literature, we did not find any researchers who proposed using either the Social Security Death Master File (SSA DMF) or the National Center for Health Statistics' Death Index File (NCHS DIF) as administrative records that potentially could be used via "record linkage" processes (see, e.g., Ericksen and Kadane 1986; Hogan 1993; Judson 2004; Krotki 1977; Madrian and Lefgren 1999; Wolter 1986; Statistics Finland 2004) to identify foreign-born decedents who were not authorized to be in the United States. If the deaths (by age and sex) of the unauthorized foreign-born population can be estimated from this process, then it may be possible that they could be used in conjunction with data derived from life tables that describe the mortality regime(s) for the unauthorized foreign-born population(s) to estimate the numbers of the unauthorized foreign-born using a variation of the "vital statistics" method for estimating population (Bogue 1950). As an example of how this might work, suppose deaths for a given period have been matched between the SSA DMF and the NCHS DIF and that the un-matched cases represent a reasonable estimate of deaths to the unauthorized foreign-born population (by age and sex). If we have a life table that provides a good representation of this population, we can apply the method of Greville (see, e.g., Kintner 2004) for estimating "${}_nL_x$" to get an estimate of the unauthorized foreign-born population aged x to $x + n$ at a given point in time as follows:

$${}_nP_x = [({}_nd_x)/({}_nD_x/{}_nL_x)]$$

where

${}_nP_x$ The (estimated) unauthorized foreign-born population aged x to $x + n$;
${}_nd_x$ Estimated deaths of unauthorized foreign-born aged x to x + n (from the SSA DMF/NCHS DIF matching process);
${}_nD_x$ Deaths in the life table to the population reaching age x (l_x) before reaching age l_{x+n};
${}_nL_x$ Life table population aged x to $x + n$.

These age-based estimates of the unauthorized foreign-born population could be done by sex and geographic area and compared to estimates generated from other methods. A variation on this proposed method is to use the "Vital Rates" Method (Bogue 1950) to estimate this same population. This would be accomplished as follows:

$${}_nP_x = {}_nd_x / {}_nm_x$$

where

${}_nP_x$ The (estimated) unauthorized foreign-born population aged x to $x + n$;
${}_nd_x$ Estimated deaths of unauthorized foreign-born aged x to $x + n$ (from the SSA DMF/NCHS DIF matching process);
${}_nm_x$ The death rate for those aged x to $x + n$ in a population believed to represent the mortality to which the unauthorized foreign-born population is subject.

It is, of course, a research question as to the efficacy of either of the two variations of this proposed method, given that the SSA DMF and NCHS DIF files can be obtained for this purpose and processed in a cost-effective manner and that record linkage error is low. However, if these conditions were met then these two variations could be used for De jure or De facto estimates, depending on the use of "place of residence" or "place of occurrence" death records.

Estimating the Foreign Born Using Specialized Survey and Related Statistical Methods[4]

Although Grieco (2003), among others, has called for a large-scale post-census survey on the foreign-born (presumably by the US Census Bureau), neither has such a survey been undertaken nor is one (to the best of our knowledge) planned. Moreover, few surveys have been undertaken to specifically isolate the illegal

[4] Some of the material in this section is adapted from Golden (2008).

immigrant population. Most information on illegal immigrants in the workforce has been generated from Census Bureau data, using, for example, the residual method, as has been discussed. Heer (1990) describes one of the early uses of a survey-based method to estimate the size of the unauthorized foreign-born, in this case, Los Angeles County, California. The method that he describes uses a combination of 1980 census data and the results of a survey conducted in Los Angeles County in 1980 and 1981. A sample was selected from babies born in Los Angeles County who had a mother or father of Mexican origin. The survey included questions about the legal status of the baby's parents and certain other relatives. The resulting estimates of unauthorized Mexican immigrants are for males aged 18–44 years and females aged 18–39 years. Heer and Passel (1987) compared the estimates obtained from this survey to estimates they derived from estimates of the unauthorized foreign-born obtained from the 1980 census using a residual method (Warren and Passel 1987; Passel and Woodrow 1984). Specifically, Heer and Passel (1987) derived estimates by age, sex, and period of entry for persons born in Mexico and living in Los Angeles County.

Heer followed up with a survey jointly conducted in the fall of 1994 by the University of Southern California and El Colegio de la Frontera Norte (COLEF), an academic institution located in Tijuana, Mexico. From this survey, he obtained estimates of the legal status of the children of unauthorized Mexican immigrants in Los Angeles County, California. Using data from this same survey in conjunction with the March 1994 and 1995 Current Population Surveys, Marcelli and Heer (1998) estimated the number of unauthorized Mexican immigrants residing in Los Angeles County, and compared their use of seven welfare programs with that of other non-U.S. citizens and U.S. citizens.

In 1991, DaVanzo et al. (1994) conducted a pilot study, the "Los Angeles Community Survey of Salvadorans and Filipinos." The survey was able to obtain information from 11-year-old census data to target high-concentration sample areas; it successfully recruited and trained bilingual staff; it enlisted respondents' cooperation at acceptable rates; and it elicited responses to sensitive questions, including immigration status, that are critical for developing and assessing policy. The authors concluded that costs for a similar survey conducted in selected sites across the country, though substantial, would be low compared with the potential costs that immigration may impose, or even with the costs of programs intended to address immigration issues.

Regional studies using survey data are found outside of California. Flores (1984), for example, obtained social and demographic data from a sample of parents of unauthorized children in Texas while analyzing the international ramifications of a legal case.

As another example of a specialized survey not restricted to California, Massey (1987) describes an "ethnosurvey" research approach designed to overcome the limitations of federal immigration statistics and to illuminate the social processes underlying aggregate patterns of migration. Massey (1999) evaluates the validity of the ethnosurvey as a method of demographic data collection by analyzing the representativeness of the Mexican Migration Project (MMP) as a source of information on Mexico-U.S. migration. He finds that the ethnosurvey is an accurate and reliable method of data collection and the MMP as a good source of reasonably representative data on authorized and unauthorized migration to the United States, even though it over-represents migrants in the western states and mid-sized communities.

Paradies and Barnes (2005) provide a description of a variant of dual-record population estimation (see, e.g., Krotki 1977), which relies on the availability of specific additional information to relax the assumption of perfect frame specification. This variant is applied to two remote indigenous communities in the Northern Territory of Australia, using locally available data sources. Further theoretical exploration of this method is presented along with possible applications in estimating area-enumerated populations and census coverage.

Droitcour et al. (1991) describe a an innovative survey-based method that extends "randomized response," which uses two questions, one sensitive and one not, to get at sensitive information. They call it the "item count method," in which respondents are given lists of behaviors in which the sensitive behavior is imbedded among a list of non-sensitive behaviors. Respondents indicate the number of the behaviors that apply to them rather than answering questions on the actual behaviors. Random parts of the sample receive lists with and without the sensitive behavior. Like randomized response, the item count method allows the researcher to use statistical methods to estimate the total number of people who engaged in the sensitive behavior; However, neither randomized response nor the item count method allow one to determine if a particular person engaged in the sensitive behavior. Because of this feature, both randomized response and the item count method preclude disclosure to the general public and sponsor as well as to the interviewer and other persons who may be nearby. By 1998, this method had been refined into a technique dubbed the "grouped answers" method (U.S. GAO 2006). Subsequent to 1998, U.S. GAO (1999) extended this discussion and labels the technique as the "three card method." It is intended to allow estimation of the needed statistics while maximizing response privacy and reducing "question threat."

Droitcour et al. (2001) discuss in more detail this innovative method, which they call the "three card method." They provide: (1) basic logic; (2) special features; (3) preliminary testing and results; and (4) variance costs and ways to reduce them. They also show how an immigration group that is currently of special concern—"visa overstays"— might be estimated using a version of the method.

Droitcour and Larson (2002) continue exploring the "three-card" method, which they describe as a technique that the United States Government Accountability Office (GAO) designed as a "grouped answers" approach to estimating irregular migration in a survey. The method directly estimates the number of persons in various "regular" or legal immigration status groups, indirectly estimates the number in sensitive irregular groups, while providing privacy protection. GAO created this methodology because of a lack of data; without information on immigration status, "policy researchers cannot track trends in employment or other important outcomes (such as subsequent educational attainment, income/poverty status, or family formation experience) for legal immigrants, illegal aliens, or persons of other immigration statuses.

U.S. GAO (2006) reviews the ongoing development of a potential method for obtaining such information: the "grouped answers" approach, which is a variant of the three-card approach just described. In 1998, GAO devised the approach and recommended further study. In response, the Census Bureau tested respondent acceptance and recently reported results. GAO answers four questions: (1) Is the grouped answers approach acceptable for use in a national survey of the foreign-born; (2) What further research may be needed; (3) How large a survey is needed; and (4) Are any ongoing surveys appropriate for inserting a grouped answers question series (to avoid the cost of a new survey)? For this study, GAO consulted an independent statistician and other experts, performed test calculations, obtained documents, and interviewed officials and staff at federal agencies. The Census Bureau and DHS agreed with the main findings of this report. DHHS agreed that the National Survey of Drug Use and Health is not an appropriate survey for inserting a grouped answers question. GAO finds that the grouped answers approach is acceptable to many experts and immigrant advocates, with certain conditions, such as (for some advocates) private sector data collection.

Larson (2007) describes a recent method based on the "grouped-answers" approach, which he calls the "Two-Card Follow-Up" method, because two different cards list different groups of immigration statuses and follow-up questions. Five key points of the method are: (1) The categories must be mutually exclusive and exhaustive; (2) No respondent is ever asked whether he, she, or anyone else is in a specific sensitive category (for example, illegal immigrant or "irregular migrant"; in this example, currently "unauthorized"); (3) Follow-up questions are asked of respondents; (4) Two pieces of information are separately provided by two sub-samples of respondents (completely different people—no one is shown both immigration status cards); (5) taking the two pieces of information together—like two pieces of a puzzle—allows indirect estimation of the unauthorized population, but no individual respondent (and no piece of data on an individual respondent) is ever categorized as unauthorized.

Golden (2008) applied a variant of the "two card" follow-up method to estimate the number of illegal immigrant workers on projects in the region of Washington, DC. Golden describes her application of this method as follows. Respondents are shown one of the cards in Exhibit 2; a random half of the sample is shown card 1, and the other half is shown card 2.

Continuing, Golden says that respondents are asked to pick the box that includes their current immigration status, but not to pick specific categories within the box, just the letter A, B, or C, corresponding to the box that contains their current immigration status. The percentage of illegal immigrants is calculated by subtracting the percentage that picked Box A from one card from the percentage that picked Box B from the other card and adding the percentage that picked box C from either card. This estimate includes the truly unauthorized or illegal immigrants and those with "quasi-legal" status. Both categories are affected by immigration reform and therefore, both categories are relevant to this research.

CARD 1 CARD 2

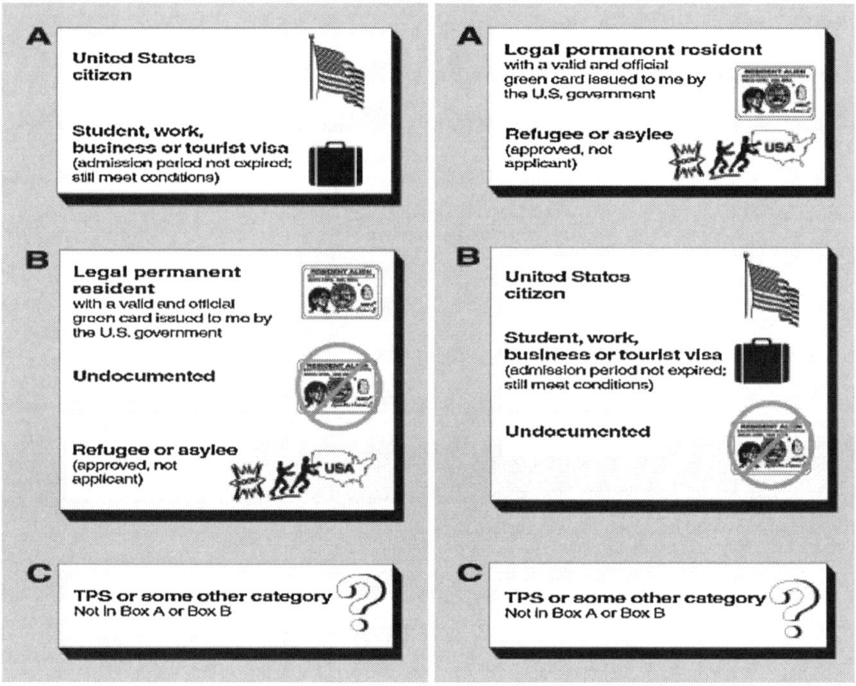

Exhibit 2 Immigration status cards

The number of truly unauthorized or illegal immigrants can be calculated by subtracting Box A from Box B, without adding Box C.

As noted by Golden (2008) and GAO (1999), among others, the basic logic behind the "Two-Card Method" is as follows. The total sample is chosen such that half of the sample is sufficient in order to generate statistically sound estimates. Half of the sample is shown card 1, and the other half of the sample is shown card 2. The half of the sample that is shown card 1 is used to estimate those respondents that are United States citizens or are present in the U.S. on a valid student, work, business, or tourist visa, i.e. those that pick Box A from card 1. The half of the sample that is shown card 2 is used to estimate those respondents that are United States citizens, are present in the U.S. on a valid student, work, business, or tourist visa, or are unauthorized immigrants, i.e. those that pick Box B. "Quasi-legal" immigrants, those that are present in the U.S. through a Temporary Protected Status, those eligible for the Deferred Enforced Departure (DED) program, Nicaraguan and Central American Relief Act beneficiaries, asylum applicants, fiancé, spouse, or child visa applicants—known as adjustment applicants, and Legal Immigrant Family Equity Act (LIFE) section 245(i) beneficiaries are estimated from those that choose Box C from either card 1 or card 2. The percentage of illegal immigrants, then, is calculated by subtracting the estimate of United States citizens and those present in the U.S. on a valid student, work, business, or tourist visa, those that picked Box A from card 1, from the estimate of United States citizens, those present in the U.S. on a valid student, work, business, or tourist visa, and unauthorized immigrants, those that picked Box B from card 2, plus the estimate of "quasi-legal" immigrants, those that picked box C from either card. The number of truly unauthorized immigrants can be calculated by subtracting Box A-card 1 from Box B-card 2, without adding Box C-card 1 or card 2.

Alternatively, Golden (2008) notes that the half of the sample that is shown card 2 may also be used to estimate those respondents that are Legal Permanent Residents (LPR's) and those that are present in the U.S. under an approved refugee or asylee status, i.e. those that pick Box A from card 2. The half of the sample that is shown card 1 may be used to estimate those respondents that are Legal Permanent Residents (LPR's), those that are present in the U.S. under an approved refugee or asylee status, and those that are unauthorized immigrants, i.e. those that pick Box B from card 1. Again, "quasi-legal" immigrants may be estimated from those that choose Box C from either card 1 or card 2. Then, the percentage of illegal immigrants would be calculated by subtracting the estimate of Legal Permanent Residents (LPR's) and those that are present in the U.S. under an approved refugee or asylee status, those that picked Box A from card 2, from the estimate of Legal Permanent Residents (LPR's), those that are present in the U.S. under an approved refugee or asylee status, and those that are unauthorized immigrants, those that picked Box B from card 1, plus the estimate of "quasi-legal" immigrants, those that picked box C from either card. The number of truly unauthorized immigrants is still calculated by subtracting Box A—card 2 from Box B—card 1, without adding Box C—card 1 or card 2.

Because the total sample is sufficient for half of the sample to produce statistically relevant estimates, it will not matter whether the Box A estimate from card 1 is subtracted from the Box B estimate from card 2 or the Box A estimate from card 2 is subtracted from the Box B estimate from card 1. Both calculations should reveal similar results.

As stated earlier, this survey method requires two representative samples of the population of interest; one is shown card 1 and the other card 2. The sensitive category of unauthorized is presented with two less sensitive categories in Box B. If respondents choose Box B, no further inquiry is made. If respondents choose Box A, which is composed of 2 less sensitive categories of immigration status, several follow-up questions are asked to be sure that the respondent has chosen Box A correctly. The follow-up questions include asking under which program they received their legal status, country of origin, year of entry, and year they acquired legal status. Box C is comprised of a less-sensitive and rare category among the sample. If respondents choose Box C, several follow-up questions are asked as well to ensure that respondents have chosen the correct category. The cards are arranged so that Box A from card 1 contains the same two less sensitive categories of immigration status appearing with the sensitive category of unauthorized in Box B of card 2.

Limitations of this method include the necessity to conduct the survey via in-person interview and the large sample required to obtain accurate estimates. Approximately 2,000 respondents are needed for an estimate of the percentage unauthorized with a 90% confidence interval of plus or minus 4 percentage points, assuming 50% of the respondents are unauthorized. If the assumption is that only 30% of the population of interest is unauthorized, then 2,500 survey respondents are required for the same confidence interval (GAO 2006).

Another method used in direct survey of the foreign-born for the express purpose of determining immigration status is the Residency Status Assignment based on answers to a series of questions (Marcelli and Lowell 2005). In this method, residency status is assigned to respondent based on answers to a series of questions. While the question of being unauthorized is never asked outright, the status of immigration is implied by the answers to these questions.

In concluding this section on survey-based methods, we note that "capture–recapture" methods are used to estimate wildlife populations (Besbeas et al. 2002; Williams et al. 2002). The same ideas can be applied to human populations using prior census counts, surveys, administrative records, and combinations of the preceding data sources (Alho 1994; Chandrasekaran and Deming 1949). Wolter (1990), for example, describes methods of estimating population size based on capture–recapture data. The methods exploit knowledge of the sex ratio, males per female, and permit "estimability" even when both time of sampling and marking affect "catchability." Scheuren and Lancaster (1978) used this type of technique in constructing a dual system estimate of unauthorized persons.

Another intriguing possibility for estimating characteristics of the foreign-born population by legal status is that of modeling using existing survey data. In Judson (2006), the "SIPP Imputation model" used a question on the 2004 panel data on migrant legal status to "impute" such statuses on the ACS microdata. Because the survey question was sensitive, it is likely that "social desirability bias" (Nederhof 2006) played a role in the response. Upon tabulation of the imputations, this model generated the lowest level of unauthorized of any of the methods tested, likely reflecting this presumed response bias. However, a possible method of "correcting" for the response bias could be developed. This would involve raking the individual responses to external control totals developed by other methods, if the external control totals are believed superior for totals. After the raking, the imputation model would represent the *interiordistribution* of the data set, with the *exterior distribution* controlled.

A final area described by Judson (2006) that has just been examined recently is that of modeling the legal status distribution using cluster analysis or latent class analysis (McCutcheon 1987). Preliminary tests comparing distributions of the foreign born by clusters with distributions generated by residual methods (unpublished) suggest that clustering and/or latent class methods may have great promise in distributing the non-naturalized foreign-born population into "lawful resident" and "residual" categories (Judson 2006). It remains to be seen whether the refugee/asylee and nonimmigrants (a/k/a legal temporary) populations are sufficiently distinct from the above two categories to admit a three/four cluster or three/four class solution. It also remains to be seen whether the clustering solutions would need external control totals as appears to be the case with the SIPP Imputation approach.

An Evaluation of Data and Methods for Estimating the Foreign Born

In this section, the evaluation of methods for estimating the foreign-born is organized into two areas: (1) data; and (2) methods. Before proceeding, however, we first cover the conceptual framework and major criteria used in the evaluation.

Evaluation Criteria Description

Like most other methods for generating population estimates (see, e.g., Bryan 2004), it has been possible to evaluate methods for estimating the foreign-born in total by using decennial census counts (admitting, that the decennial census counts stem from the sample-based "long form"). This, however, changes in 2010, when the Census Bureau abandons the long form and uses the ACS as a substitute. Thus, the ACS will be the future "gold standard" against which methods for estimating the foreign-born are evaluated. With this new gold standard comes the difference in residency rules used by the traditional "short form" decennial census (De jure) and the ACS (De facto) and the fact that the ACS is then controlled to numbers that use the same residency rule as the decennial census (De jure).

When it comes to evaluating methods for estimating the foreign-born by status, particularly those who are unauthorized, there is no "gold standard." Thus, traditional frameworks and criteria used to evaluate population estimates in general require some modification because they inherently assume the presence of a gold standard. However, even though decennial census data provide the most convenient and accurate standard against which to evaluate population estimation methods, there always have been several important considerations that were taken into account before estimates are compared with census values. First, there was often a tendency to assume that earlier and later censuses are completely consistent, but such consistency cannot be taken for granted. Second, subnational areas often differ in geography and populations covered, and census definitions may have changed as well. Third, where a method was based on a past census that differs from a more recent census against which estimates resulting from the method in question were compared, in any significant way, an accurate evaluation would be compromised.

All of this leads up to the point that comparisons of estimates resulting from different methods against the census have to be considered "measures of difference" rather than "measures of error" because it is virtually impossible to precisely determine the degree to which error in the census and error in the estimate contribute to the overall difference.

Similarly, it is important to note that a direct "method-to-method" comparison is rarely possible when attempting to make a population estimate. Often, what might be the most accurate method may not be practicable due to excessive time, cost and resources. Other hindrances may include unavailability or inconsistency of necessary data. Furthermore, it will be seen, certain methods are better suited to particularly large or small areas of geography. While a certain method may generate "good results" at a national level, they may be wholly inadequate for other levels of geography. Thus the amount of resources available, the level of geography as well as historical accuracy of each method must always be considered.

Without question, an estimate should be accurate, but accuracy is not the only criterion by which an estimate should be judged. Following the argument presented by Swanson and Tayman (1995), we suggest that attention be focused on the broader concept of utility. As alluded to earlier, there are many methods that in principle can be used to estimate a population, and improvements are a regular feature of these methods. Further, there is a wide range of decision-making situations in which population estimates are used. It follows, therefore, that no method should be universally judged to be superior to others and, by the same token, neither should any method be judged universally inferior to all others. We suggest instead, that relative to a given use, utility is gained by selecting a method that provides a sufficient amount of information for the purpose(s) at hand, while keeping cost and time to a minimum. In the case of an estimate, the sufficiency of the information provided is judged on the ability of using it to make good decisions. So, if an estimate is produced at minimal cost but provides timely information sufficient to make good decisions, then it has high utility. If an estimate does not meet these conditions then it has low utility. An important underlying component of sufficiency is "transparency." That is, the ability of a decision-maker to understand how an estimate was done so that he or she can determine if the assumptions, methods, and data are reasonable.

However, some criteria do apply, including continuity; timeliness of information; refinement; production; cost, and replication. Generally speaking, these criteria can be applied to data and methods, topics to which we now turn.

Evaluation of Data

Schmidley and Robinson (2003) evaluated CPS nativity data collected between January 1994 and December 2002. Where feasible, they compare these data with data from other sources. They incorporate a limited amount of the information found in "How Well Does the Current Population Survey Measure the Foreign-Born Population in the United States?" which evaluated the March Annual Social and Economic Supplement (ASEC) nativity data 1994–1997. The current paper extends the period to 2002 and includes information about the monthly or basic survey.

Skeldon (1987) identifies and describes the main issues to be resolved when designing questions and strategies to collect migration-related data. The strengths and weaknesses of the various approaches are assessed in the light of the data collected by countries in the Asia-Pacific region during the 1980 round of censuses. In the context of the developing countries of the region, the author argues that higher quality and more useful migration data can be captured through questions on last place of previous residence and duration of residence in De facto-based censuses. Variations of, and amplifications to, this approach are considered.

Fawcett and Arnold (1987) argue that surveys provide an effective method for studies of the complex processes that underlie spatial mobility. They identify and discuss eight advantages of surveys that are related to research design and seven advantages that are related to research content. Deficiencies and disadvantages of surveys are also reviewed. Suggestions are made for improving surveys of international migration through better samples and attention to different points in a migration system.

Massey (1987) describes a research approach designed to overcome the limitations of federal immigration statistics and to illuminate the social processes underlying aggregate patterns of migration. He argues that the principal weaknesses of existing data sources are that they under-enumerate and imperfectly measure unauthorized migration; they do not reflect the widespread circularity of modern international movements; they omit variables central to the immigration process; and their cross-sectional collection and tabulation precludes the analysis of immigration as a dynamic process. The ethnosurvey is a research design that ameliorates these problems through five specific design features: multi-method data collection, representative multi-site sampling, multilevel data compilation, life history collection, and parallel sampling. These design features are described, justified, and tied to the broader methodological literature in social science. The ethnosurvey design is illustrated by its recent application to study Mexican migration to the United States, and empirical evidence is presented to show how it corrects the limitations of federal data on immigration.

In a subsequent paper, Massey (1999) evaluates the validity of his proposed ethnosurvey as a method of demographic data collection by analyzing the representativeness of the Mexican Migration Project (MMP) as a source of information on Mexico–U.S. migration. After briefly delineating the philosophy, structure, and organization of the MMP's ethnosurvey design, he describes MMP's public use dataset as well as Mexico's Encuesta Nacional de la Dinamica Demografica (ENADID) as a benchmark for its systematic evaluation. He finds that although the MMP over-represents migrants in the western states and mid-sized communities, it yields a relatively accurate and valid profile of migrants to the United States. A comparison of multivariate models estimated using MMP and ENADID data suggests that whereas the former's sampling errors are small and yield biases that are substantively unimportant, the latter's potential for specification error and selection bias may seriously compromise results. Massey concludes that his comparison thus validates the ethnosurvey as an accurate and reliable method of data collection and the MMP as a good source of reasonably representative data on authorized and unauthorized migration to the United States.

Evaluation of Methods

In this section, we evaluate methods under each of the major headings used to organize the techniques for estimating the foreign-born (by status): (1) residual; (2) administrative records; (3) specialized survey; and (4) other. We subdivide the residual method into those that are stock-based and those that are flow-based, and note that the residual method is by nature "indirect," while the other three approaches attempt to measure the characteristics and legal status of the foreign born by "direct" means. We evaluate "assumptions" in addition to inherent strengths and weaknesses.

Stock-Based Residual Methods

These methods utilize survey data, census data, or a combination of the two as primary data sources. The (long form) Decennial Census, CPS, SIPP, and, now, the ACS, all have been used. The underlying assumption for each of them is that sample precision is adequate and that non-sampling errors are minimal relative to the measurement of legal status of the foreign born. Another assumption specific to this method noted by Judson (2006) is that the assignment algorithm accurately measures visa, LPR, and naturalization requirements. Also, the assignment is "100% assignment," which assumes that everyone with the same characteristics, i.e. matching certain visa requirements, has the same status.

As has been noted earlier, the Decennial Census, CPS, and SIPP, on the one hand, use the De jure rule of residency while the ACS uses what amounts to a De facto residency rule. However, when the micro-level ACS data are aggregated to geographic areas, they are controlled to numbers produced for these areas by the Census Bureau's annual population estimates program. It does not appear to be the case that ACS data so controlled are used in the stock-based residual methods, which rely on micro-level data. If this is the case, then comparing estimates made by the residual methods relying on the census, CPS, and SIPP with those made using strictly ACS data will yield differences based in part on the different residence rules. This may not be a huge issue at the national level, but at sub-state levels, the effects of these different residency rules could be substantial. Where ACS micro-level data are used in conjunction with micro-level data from the CPS, SIPP, or the (2000) census, it is highly likely that mismatches occur.

These methods have a number of limitations and strengths. A major limitation is the fact that none of these data sources contain direct questions on legal status, which means that the components are constructed from estimating or imputing legal status. Another important limitation assumes that the information used from the microdata actually reflect the visa, LPR, and citizenship criteria. Finally, as noted by Judson (2006), each case matching certain characteristics is allocated as either meeting or not meeting the criteria for the legal status and this may be neither accurate nor necessarily appropriate.

However, CPS, SIPP and ACS microdata represents a strength for both Census Bureau staff and external researchers holding clearances to access micro-level data, because the U.S. Census Bureau is not an administrative or enforcement agency and does not have regular access to other agencies' data.

Another strength is that these methods are flexible. They can easily be adapted to accommodate three important scenarios. First, the requirements for the visa, citizenship, and LPR statuses themselves may change and change very quickly, for instance, by a policy-setting agency. The algorithm method is easily changed to meet these new conditions. Second, the algorithms can be reproduced under alternate assumptions regarding the matching between the microdata information and visa or LPR criteria.

Depending on the micro-level base data, the ACS on the one hand or the Decennial Census and CPS, on the other, these methods will produce estimates of either the De facto or De jure population, respectively. If ACS micro-level data are used in conjunction with micro-level data from the other sources, then it is not clear if the result is more "De jure than De facto", or vice versa.

Flow-Based Residual Methods

Many of the same assumptions just mentioned are also pertinent to this method and depending on the use of the Decennial Census or the ACS, the resulting estimates are either of the De jure or De facto population, respectively.

A major assumption underlying this approach is that the components of population change are closely approximated by measuring change in selected administrative or survey data sources. In order to apply the model, Census Bureau demographers estimate each component of population change and legal status category separately. In addition, this method makes the (crucial) assumption that the administrative and survey data that are used to construct demographic flows are comparable; that is, that the time reference, time frame for data production, and concepts can be appropriately compared to one another.

Using data to approximate the measures of components of change that can be updated on an annual basis could prove to be invaluable as this would be more representative of the process that is actually happening in the population. However, the assumption that there is available data that closely approximates the measure of each of the components of change within a particular legal status category may prove to be a difficulty and should be viewed as potential and important limitation to the use of this method of estimation. If certain components of the equation cannot be accurately approximated by the data, then it is possible that the residual category will be significantly overestimated, while other legal status categories will be underestimated, since the sum of all legal status categories at time t must be equal to the total foreign born population at time t.

Another issue in regard to the residual method in general is that it tends to cumulate error. As a concrete example, recall again the equation due to Deardorff and Blumerman (2001) that was presented earlier:

$$\mathrm{FB} = [L - [M + E] + T + R],$$

where,

FB	Foreign-born population;
L	Legal Immigrants;
M	Mortality to legal immigrants;
E	Emigration of legal immigrants;
T	Temporary (legal) migrants; and
R	Residual foreign-born (unauthorized and quasi-legal migrants).

Rearranging the terms yields

$$R = \mathrm{FB} - L + M + E - T.$$

If each of the elements on the right-hand side of the equation is measured with some level of error, e (a reasonable assumption), then the residual estimate becomes

$$\begin{aligned} R &= (\mathrm{FB} + e_{\mathrm{FB}}) - (L + e_L) + (M + e_M) + (E + e_E) - (T + e_T) \\ &= (\mathrm{FB} - L + M + E - T) + (e_{\mathrm{FB}} + e_L + e_M + e_E + e_T), \end{aligned}$$

which means

$$R - (e_{\mathrm{FB}} + e_L + e_M + e_E + e_T) = \mathrm{FB} - L + M + E - T.$$

In other words, all of the error ends up in the residual estimate. These errors may, of course, offset one another, but there is no way to gain a reliable and valid assessment of this either beforehand or after the fact. Moreover, the errors combine both sampling and non-sampling error. In regard to the sampling error, having small standard errors is critical to the development of reasonable estimates. In regard to the non-sampling error, there is no measure of standard error that allows the assessment of the effects of coverage, non-response, measurement, and recording errors. Moreover, in this implementation the residual method runs the risk of "residual error propagation" in that the term "E" is itself a residual estimate.

In general, the issue of having error accumulate in the estimate is not unique to this particular implementation of the residual method. It also applies, for example to all residual methods in principle, including the residual method for estimating net intercensal migration (Morrison et al. 2004).

Another problematic error with the variants of the residual method evaluated here is that the components tend to be functionally related. This means that an error in one component tends to introduce an error in the opposite direction in another. Unlike the situation of multi-collinearity in a multiple regression model, there is no clear way to assess this in the residual model.

Judson (2006) observes that the "slippages" between data sources is a significant limitation of this method for two reasons. First, he notes that transaction-based data have not been converted to a person-based estimate. Second, he argues that it is not clear if the major assumptions underlying the method are reasonable. This method is aimed at targeting the De jure foreign-born population by status because it uses census data.

Paradies and Barnes (2005) provide a description of a variant of dual-record population estimation (see, e.g., Marks et al. 1974; Krotki 1977), which relies on the availability of specific additional information to relax the assumption of perfect frame specification. This variant is applied to two remote indigenous communities in the Northern Territory of Australia, using locally available data sources. Further theoretical exploration of this method is presented along with possible applications in estimating area-enumerated populations and census coverage.

Suggestions

Data

Data needs can be organized into four major areas: immigration, emigration, the De jure foreign-born population and the De facto foreign-born population. Immigration data are a mess and emigration data are essentially non-existent. It is hard to understand how valid and reliable estimates of the foreign-born, whether on a De jure or De facto basis can be generated without valid and reliable information on immigration and emigration.

In addition to being collected in historical census enumerations, data on the De jure foreign-born population were collected in the modern (since 1950) decennial census enumerations and in the ACS and the SIPP. In the 1980 census, data were even collected on "temporary residents" (National Research Council, 2006a, b, p. 114). With census 2010, the decennial census will no longer be a source of these data. Given this, it is not clear what direction the CPS and the SIPP will take if they continue to exist beyond 2010. This means that the residual estimates that were produced using data from the decennial census can no longer be done unless one uses the 2000 census as a launch point. Thus, it is an open question if the ACS and SIPP can be used. These points lead to the conclusion that once 2010 rolls around, all estimates of the foreign-born will effectively be those of the De facto population, not the De jure population.

One of the first suggestions we would have made (until it was clear that there will no longer be a long form in the decennial census) was to understand the effect of the different residency rules used by the decennial census, the CPS, and the SIPP, on the one hand, and the ACS, on the other, and to take these differences into account both when comparing estimates developed from these different sources and when attempting to use elements of both in developing estimates. However, this appears to now be a moot point. Morever, it does need to be taken into account when using other data sets such as NIIS, the NCHS death and birth files, and other administrative records. Finally, in conducting special surveys aimed at directly estimating the foreign-born (by status), suggest that the type of population being estimated needs to be clearly defined. Further, it appears that using the ACS definition of residency would be more valuable than using the decennial census rules since the former leads to comparability between a specialized survey and the ACS, while the latter does not. Moreover, the ACS could be used to generate both types of estimates. Happel and Hogan (2002) as well as Smith and House (2004) provide suggestions on how this could be accomplished in terms of De jure and "temporary resident" populations and their suggestions could easily be extended to De jure and De facto populations.

Methods

The lack of a gold standard against which to compare status-based estimates of the foreign-born suggest that the only course of action to attempt to have valid and reliable estimates is to construct them from different methods and data sets that while having different strengths and weaknesses that lead to different assumptions underlying the estimates, are reasonably reliable and valid. Thus, we suggest that the existing forms of the residual, administrative records, specialized survey, and "other" methods be continued along with the exploration of new ones.

Any residual methods in the future will be based on the ACS. It is inescapable. Therefore, we suggest that they continue to be done, but that it is made clear that the ACS rules of residency are different than those found in the "short form" counts of population in the decennial census and, likely in the post-censal estimates (and projections) produced from them. In order to avoid these inconsistencies, we suggest that a uniform set of residency rules be used across all of the federal efforts. Initially, this will cause a great deal of disruption because it will represent a major break with the past. However, it makes no sense to have one major data collection method such as the "short form" decennial census using one set of rules (De jure) and the ACS using another (De facto). Given this, residual methods represent a valuable source of information on the foreign-born (by status). Methods based on the use of administrative records as well as "other" methods also provide valuable information.

We agree with Grieco (2003) who, among others, has called for a large-scale post-census survey on the foreign-born. If this is done, we suggest that the "two card" method be strongly considered because it represents a *direct* source of information on the foreign-born (by status) and, appears to be the *only* realistic way to get at direct data-based (that is, not based on modeling assumptions) estimates of the foreign-born by status.

We further suggest that the idea described earlier of using the Social Security Death Master File (SSA DMF) and the National Center for Health Statistics' Death Index File (NCHS DIF) via a "record linkage" process be pursued to identify foreign-born decedents not authorized to be in the United States. It is, as observed earlier, a research question as to the efficacy of either of the two variations of this proposed method, given that the SSA DMF and NCHS DIF files can be obtained for this purpose, processed in a cost-effective manner, and that a low level of record linkage error is found. To assess each of these three conditions, a small pilot study could be implemented. If the record linkage process yields a good estimate of deaths to the unauthorized population at a given point in time by age (geography and sex), then successive sets of the estimates can be used to generate estimates (and projections) using the principles underlying the method for estimating unauthorized immigration due to Edmonston and Michalowski (2004) that was described earlier.

Summary

Because there is no gold standard, methods for estimating the foreign-born (by status) can never be subjected to the standard evaluation process used for the general methods of population estimation (Bryan 2004; Swanson 1986, 1989, 2004). Thus, the selection of methods will be based on criteria other than accuracy, such as cost and timeliness, transparency, and so forth.

There is one general principle that has emerged from our research, and which we emphasize strongly: While the "residual" and other "indirect" methods for measuring the characteristics of the foreign-born population by legal status have had value, we believe that "direct" methods need to be cultivated to *validate* and *corroborate* the "residual" methods.

There is one approach for which statistical precision can be evaluated, namely a sample survey. If such a survey is undertaken, we believe that the "Two-Card" method should be used because it is the only technique that is aimed directly at estimating the foreign-born (by status). Moreover, it has also been tested by Golden (2008). If a large scale "two-card" survey is done, we believe it would best be accomplished by contracting the work to a non-governmental entity that has the experience and human capital to implement such a survey. The survey could be developed under a guiding body that provides overall management with either the Census Bureau, the Office of Immigration Statistics, National Science Foundation, or National Research Council, (or some combination) providing the close oversight of the survey. The actual collection and technical details could be done by a major non-government survey organization with the skills and experience to handle such an endeavor. Organizations such as ISR at the University of Michigan and NORC at the University of Chicago come to mind, among others. If this path is taken, we suggest that pilot studies similar to what is done for the Decennial Census (e.g., a series of pilots in different areas, leading up to the full dress rehearsals). While precision does not equate with accuracy in the same sense as is used for other methods of population estimation, it does a serve as a substitute, which means that estimates generated by different surveys can be compared for cost, timeliness, and precision. In gearing up for such a survey, we suggested earlier that the lead Federal agency work with the NAS and potential contractors (e.g., ISR and NORC) to develop a plan and as it turns out, it appears NSF has awarded such a contract to NORC. In addition, we advise that careful attention be paid to the type of population being estimated and that rules of residency be used that are consistent with the ACS.

"Modeling" approaches to estimating the characteristics of the foreign-born population also appear to have merit in this context. Not only would they provide a model-based uncertainty measure, but the data sets currently exist and the development of appropriate models would be highly cost-effective, as they would require no new data collection activities, only analysis of the extant data sets. If Federal agencies determine that such models' output would be too politically sensitive, then other think tanks or universities can step up to the plate.

Acknowledgments The authors are grateful for comments from Eric Larson, Enrico Marcelli, Jenny Van Hook, Ed Spar, Fred Cavanaugh, Karen Woodrow-Lafield, and an anonymous reviewer. Funding for work that laid the foundation for this paper was provided to David swanson by the U.S. Census Bureau under an omnibus contract with Sabre Systems, Inc.

References

Ahmed, B., & Robinson, J. G. (1994). Estimates of emigration of the foreign-born population: 1980–1990. Population Division Working Paper No. 9. Washington, DC: U.S. Census Bureau. Retrieved September 2008 from http://www.census.gov/population/www/techpap.html

Alho, J. (1994). Analysis of sample-based capture–recapture experiments. *Journal of Official Statistics*, *10*, 245–256

Bean, F., Corona, R., Tuiran, R., & Woodrow-Lafield, K. (1998). Quantification of migration between Mexico and the United States. In *Migration between Mexico and the United States: Binational study. Thematic chapters*, *Mexico–United States binational migration study* (Vol. I, pp. 1–90). Mexican Ministry of Foreign Affairs and U.S. Commission on Immigration Reform. Retrieved April 2008 from http://www.utexas.edu/lbj/uscir/binpapers/v1-1bean.pdf

Bean, F., King, A., & Passel, J. (1983). The number of illegal migrants of Mexican origin in the United States: Sex-ratio based estimates of 1980. *Demography*, *20*, 99–109

Besbeas, P., Freeman, S. N., Morgan, B. J. T., & Catchpole, E. A. (2002). Integrating mark–recapture–recovery and census data to estimate animal abundance and demographic parameters. *Biometrics*, *58*, 540–547

Bhaskur, R., Rastogi, S., & Kennedy-Puthoff, A. (2008). Foreign-born emigration: Estimates and rates. Paper submitted for presentation at the annual meeting of the Population Association of American, New Orleans, LA. Retrieved May 2008 from http://paa2008.princeton.edu/download.aspx?submissionId=80709

Bogue, D. (1950). A technique for making extensive population estimates. *Journal of the American Statistical Association*, *45*, 191–193

Brass, W. A. (1968). *The demography of tropical Africa*. Princeton: Princeton University Press

Bryan, T. (2004). Population estimates. In J. Siegel & D. Swanson (Eds.), *The methods and materials of demography* (2nd ed., pp. 523–560). New York: Elsevier Academic Press

Camarota, S., & Capizzano, J. (2004). *Assessing the quality of data collected on the foreign born: An evaluation of the American Community Survey (ACS), pilot and full study finding*. Unpublished report. Sabre Systems, Inc. Available Online, http://www.sabresystems.com/whitepapers/CIS_whitepaper.pdf, last accessed, 2008

Capps, R., Rosenblum, M., & Fix, M. (2009). Immigrants and health reform: What's really at stake? Retrieved December 2010 from http://www.migrationpolicy.org/pubs/healthcare-Oct09.pdf

Cassidy, R. (2004a). *Involuntary and voluntary migrant algorithm*. Retrieved April 2008 from https://www.sabresystems.com/whitepapers/AMS_Deliverable_3_020305.pdf

Cassidy, R. (2004b). *Involuntary and voluntary migrant estimates*. Retrieved April 2008 from https://www.sabresystems.com/whitepapers/AMS_Deliverable_5_020305.pdf

Chandrasekaran (Chandra Sekar), C., & Deming, W. E. (1949). On a method of estimating birth and death rates and the extent of registration. *Journal of the American Statistical Association, 44*, 101–115

Costanzo, J., Davis, C., Irazi, C., Goodkind, D., & Ramirez, R. (2001). Evaluating components of international migration: The residual foreign-born. (Population Division Working Paper #61) (December 2001) U.S. Census Bureau. Retrieved August 2008 from http://www.census.gov/population/www/documentation/twps0061.html

DaVanzo, J., Hawes-Dawson, J., Valdez, R. B., Vernez, G., Andrews, C., Levitan, B., et al. (1994). *Surveying Immigrant Communities: Policy Imperatives and Technical Challenges*. Santa Monica: RAND.

Deardorff, K., & Blumerman, L. (2001). Evaluating components of international migration: Estimates of the foreign-born by migrant status in 2000. Population Division Working Paper No. 58. Washington, DC: U.S. Census Bureau

Devlin, K. (2008). *The unfinished game: Pascal, fermat and the seventeenth-century letter that made the world modern*. New York: Perseus Books Group, Basic Books

Donato, K., Durand, J., & Massey, D. (1992). Stemming the tide? Assessing the deterrent effects of the Immigration Reform and Control Act. *Demography, 29*(2), 139–157

Droitcour, J., Caspar, R., Ezzati, T., Hubbard, M., Parsley, T., & Visscher, W. (1991). The Item Count Technique as a Method of Indirect Questioning: A Review of its Development and a Case Study Application. In P. Biemer, R. Groves, L. Lyberg, N. Mathiowetz, & S. Sudman (Eds.), *Measurement Errors in Surveys* (pp. 85–210). New York City, NY: John Wiley & Sons.

Droitcour, J., & Larson, E. (2002). An innovative technique for asking sensitive questions: The three-card method. *Bulletin de Mèthodologie Sociologique, 75*, 5–23

Droitcour, J., Larson, E., & Scheuren, F. (2001). The Three-Card Method: Estimating Sensitive Survey Items–With Permanent Anonymity of Response. In: *Proceedings of the Survey Research methods Section, American Statistical Association*. Alexandria, VA: American Statistical Association.

Edmonston, B., & Michalowski, M. (2004). International migration. In J. Siegel & D. A. Swanson (Eds.), *The methods and materials of demography* (2nd ed., pp. 455–492). San Diego: Elsevier Academic Press

Eldridge, H. (1947). Problems and methods of estimating post-censal population. *Social Forces, 24*, 41–46

Ericksen, E. P., & Kadane, J. B. (1986). Using administrative lists to estimate census omissions. *Journal of Official Statistics, 2*, 397–414

Espenshade, T., & Acevedo, D. (1995). Migrant cohort size, enforcement effort, and the apprehension of unauthorized aliens. *Population Research and Policy Review, 14*, 145–172

Fawcett, J., & Arnold, F. (1987). The role of surveys in the study of international migration: An appraisal. *International Migration Review, 21*(4), 1523–1540

Fernandez, E. (1995). Using Analytical Techniques to Evaluate the 1990 Census Coverage of Young Hispanics. Population Division Technical Working Paper No. 11. Washington, DC: U.S. Census Bureau

Flanagan, W. (2002). *Urban sociology* (4th ed.). Boston: Allyn and Bacon

Flores, E. (1984). Research on Unauthorized Immigrants and Public Policy: A Study of the Texas School Case. *International Migration Review 18*(3), Special Issue: 505-523.

Fortuny, K., Capps, R., & Passel, J. (2007). The characteristics of unauthorized immigrants in California, Los Angeles County, and the United States. Washington, DC: The Urban Institute. Retrieved April 2008 from http://www.urban.org/UploadedPDF/411425 Characteristics Immigrants.pdf

Gerstle, G. (2008). The immigrant as a threat to American security: A historical perspective. In E. Barkan, H. Diner, & A. Kraut (Eds.), *From arrival to incorporation: Migrants to the U.S. in a global era* (pp. 217–245). New York City: New York University Press

Gibbs, J., Harper, G., Rubin, M., & Shin, H. (2003). Evaluating components of international migration: Native-born emigrants. Population Division Working Paper No. 63. Retrieved March 2008 from http://www.census.gov/population/www/techpap.html

Goldberg, H. (1974). *Estimates of emigration and illegal entry into the United States, 1969–1970, by the residual method.* Center for Population Research, Georgetown University, unpublished manuscript)

Golden, S. K. (2008). *Immigration and construction: an analysis of the impact of immigration on construction project costs.* Unpublished Ph.D. Dissertation, Department of Civil and Environmental Engineering, University of Maryland

Grieco, E. (2003). Census 2010 and the foreign born: Averting the data crisis. *Migration Policy Institute Policy Brief, 1*(February): 1–11

Grieco, E. (2004). *Estimates of the non-immigrant population in the United States*: 2004. Washington, DC: Department of Homeland Security, Office of Immigration Statistics

Hansen, K., & Bachu, A. (1995). The foreign-born population: 1994. Current population reports P20-486. Washington, DC: U.S. Census Bureau

Happel, S., & Hogan, T. (2002). Counting snowbirds: The importance of and the problems with estimating seasonal populations. *Population Research and Policy Review, 21*, 227–240

Hauser, P., & Tepping, B. (1944). Evaluation of census wartime population estimates and of predictions of postwar population prospects for metropolitan areas. *American Sociological Review, 9*, 473–480

Heer, D. (1979). What is the annual flow of unauthorized Mexican immigrants to the United States? *Demography, 16*, 417–424

Heer, D. (1990). *Unauthorized Mexicans in the United States. Arnold and Caroline Rose Monograph Series of the American Sociological Association.* New York City, NY: Cambridge University Press.

Heer, D., & Passel, J. (1987). Comparison of two methods for estimating the number of unauthorized Mexican adults in Los Angeles County. *International Migration Review, 21*(4), 1446–1473

Hill, K. (1985). Indirect approaches to assessing stocks and flows of migrants. In D. Levine, K. Hill, & R. Warren (Eds.), *Immigration statistics: A story of neglect* (pp. 205–224). Washington, DC: National Academy Press

Hill, K. (1987). New approaches to the estimation of migration flows from census and administrative data. *International Migration Review, 21*(4), 1279–1303

Hoefer, M., Rytina, N., & Baker, B. C. (2009). Estimates of the unauthorized immigrant population residing in the United States: January 2008. Retrieved July 2009 from http://www.dhs.gov/xlibrary/assets/statistics/publications/ois_ill_pe_2008.pdf

Hoefer, M., Rytina, N., & Campbell, C. (2006). Estimates of the unauthorized immigrant population residing in the United States: January 2005. Retrieved July 2008 from http://www.uscis.gov/graphics/shared/statistics/publications/ILL_PE_2005.pdf

Hoefer, M., Rytina, N., & Campbell, C. (2007). *Estimates of the unauthorized immigrant population residing in the United States*: *January* 2006. Washington, DC: U.S. Department of Homeland Security, Office of Immigration Statistics

Hogan, H. (1993). The 1990 post-enumeration survey: Operation and results. *Journal of the American Statistical Association*, *88*, 1047–1060

Judson, D. (2004). Evaluating the potential for an administrative records census. Presentation given at the Cathie Marsh Research Centre, University of Manchester, Manchester, England, 2nd November

Judson, D. (2006). Memorandum for E. Lamas (21 September): Subject: Preliminary results and evaluation of experimental estimates of the foreign-born population by legal status. US Census Bureau. Retrieved March 2008 from http://wikileaks.org/wiki/US Census Bureau Estimates of Unauthorized Persons

Judson, D. H. (2007). Information integration for constructing social statistics: History, theory, and ideas toward a research programme. *Journal of the Royal Statistical Society*, *170*, 483–501

Judson, D., & Popoff, C. (2004). Appendix C, Selected General Methods. In: Siegel and D. Swanson (eds.) The Methods and Materials of Demography, 2nd Edition. Amsterdam, The Netherlands: Elsevier Academic Press, pp. 677-732

Kintner, H. (2004). The life table. In J. Siegel & D. A. Swanson (Eds.), *The methods and materials of demography* (2nd ed., pp. 301–340). San Diego: Elsevier Academic Press

Krotki, K. J. (1977). *Developments in dual system estimation population size and growth.* Edmonton: University of Alberta Press

Lancaster, C., & Scheuren, F. (1978). Counting the uncountable illegals: Some initial statistical speculations employing capture–recapture techniques. In *Proceedings of the social statistics section*, 1977: *Part* I (pp. 530–535). Alexandria: American Statistical Association

Larsen, L. (2004). The foreign-born population in the United States: 2003. Current population reports P20-555. Washington, DC: U.S. Census Bureau

Larson, E. (2007). Estimating Irregular Migration in a Survey: The Two Card Follow-up Method. Sixth Coordination Meeting on International Migration. New York, NY: Population Division, Department of Economic and Social Affairs, United Nations. UN/POP /MIG-6CM/2007/01

Long, J. (1993). An overview of population estimation methods. In D. Bogue, E. Arriaga, & D. Anderton (Eds.), *Readings in population research methodology* (Vol. 5, pp. 20-1–20-5). Chicago: United Nations Population Funds and Social Development Center

Madrian, B., & Lefgren, L. (1999). An approach to longitudinally matching the current population survey. NBER Technical Working Paper No. 247. National Bureau of Economic Research. November. Retrieved January 2008 from http://papers.nber.org/papers/T0247

Malone, N., Beluja, K., Costanzo, J., & Davis, C. (2003). The foreign born population: 2000. Census 2000 brief. Washington, DC: U.S. Census Bureau

Marcelli, E., & Heer, D. (1998). The unauthorized Mexican immigrant population and welfare in Los Angeles County: A comparative statistical analysis. *Sociological Perspectives*, *41*(2), 279–302

Marcelli, E. A., & Lowell, B. L. (2005). Transnational twist: Pecuniary remittances and socioeconomic integration among authorized and unauthorized Mexican immigrants in Los Angeles County. *International Migration Review*, *39*(1), 69–102

Marks, E., Seltzer, W., & Krotki, K. (1974). *Population growth estimation*: *A Handbook of Vital Statistics Estimation.* New York City: The Population Council

Martin, E., & Burke, C. (2010). Health reform: What is the future for undocumented immigrants? Retrieved December 2010 from http://healthaffairs.org/blog/2010/10/15/health-reform-what-is-the-future-for-undocumented-aliens/

Massey, D. (1987). The ethnosurvey in theory and practice. *International Migration Review*, *21*, 1498–1522

Massey, D. (1999). Why Does Immigration Occur? A Theoretical Synthesis. In C. Hirschman, P. Kasinitz, & J. DeWind (Eds.), *The Handbook of International Migration: The American Experience* (pp. 34–52). New York, NY: Russell Sage Foundation.

McCutcheon, A. (1987). *Latent class analysis. Quantitative applications in the social sciences* (series no. 64). Thousand Oaks: Sage Publications

Morrison, P., Bryan, T., & Swanson, D. A. (2004). Internal migration and short-distance mobility. In J. Siegel & D. A. Swanson (Eds.), *The methods and materials of demography* (2nd ed., pp. 493–521) San Diego: Elsevier Academic Press

National Research Council (2006a). *Once, only once, and in the right place: Residence rules in the decennial census*. Washington, DC: National Academies Press

National Research Council (2006b). *Multiple origins, uncertain destinies: Hispanics and the American future*. Washington, DC: National Academies Press

National Research Council (2007). *Using the American community survey: Benefits and challenges*. Washington, DC: National Academies Press

Nederhof, A. (2006). Methods of coping with social desirability bias: A review. *European Journal of Social Psychology, 15*(3), 263–280

North, D., & Houston, M. (1976). *The characteristics and role of illegal aliens in the U.S. labor market: An exploratory study*. Washington, DC: Linton

Orrenius, P., & Zavodny, M. (2006). Did 9/11 worsen the job prospects of hispanic immigrants? Research Department Working Paper 0508. Dallas: Federal Reserve Bank of Dallas. Retrieved May 2008 from http://209.85.173.104/search?q=cache:QS902hgenocJ:www.dallasfed.org/research/papers/2005/wp0508.pdf+review+passel+2005+%22Estimates+of+the+Size+and+Characteristics+of+the+Unauthorized%22&hl=en&ct=clnk&cd=9&gl=us

Paradies, Y., & Barnes, T. (2005). A new variant of dual-record population estimation with an application in remote indigenous communities. *Journal of Population Research, 22*(2), 119–139

Passel, J. (2005). *Estimates of the size and characteristics of the unauthorized population*. Washington, DC: Pew Hispanic Center

Passel, J. (2006). *The size and characteristics of the unauthorized migrant population in the U.S.: Estimates based on the March 2005 current population survey*. Washington, DC: Pew Hispanic Center

Passel, J. (2007). Unauthorized migrants in the United States: Estimates, methods, and characteristics. Working Paper No. 57, Organization for Economic Cooperation and Development. Paris: Organization for Economic Cooperation and Development. Retrieved May 2008 from http://www.oecd.org/dataoecd/41/25/39264671.pdf

Passel, J., Van Hook, J., Bean, F. (2004). Estimates of the legal and unauthorized foreign-born population for the United States and selected states, based on census 2000. Arlington: Immigration White Papers, Sabre Systems. Retrieved December 2007 from http://www.sabresystems.com/sd_whitepapers_immigration.asp

Passel, J., & Woodrow, K. (1984). Geographic distribution of unauthorized immigrants: Estimates of unauthorized aliens counted in the 1980 census by state. *International Migration Review, 18*, 642–671

Passel, J., & Woodrow, K. (1987). Change in the unauthorized alien population in the United States, 1979–1983. *International Migration Review, 21*(4), 1304–1334

Popoff, C., & Judson, D. (2004). Some methods of estimation for statistically underdeveloped areas. In J. Siegel & D. Swanson (Eds.), *The methods and materials of demography* (2nd ed., pp. 603–641). Amsterdam: Elsevier Academic Press.

Robinson, J. G., Ahmed, B., Das Gupta, P., & Woodrow, K. (1993). A. Estimation of population coverage in the 1990 United States census based on demographic analysis. *Journal of the American Statistical Association, 88*(423), 1061–1079

Rytina, N. (2004). *Estimates of the Legal Permanent Resident Population and Population Eligible to Naturalize in 2002*. http://www.uscis.gov/graphics/shared/statistics/publications/LPRest2002.pdf

Rytina, N. (2005). *Estimates of the Legal Permanent Resident Population and Population Eligible to Naturalize in 2003*. http://www.uscis.gov/graphics/shared/statistics/publications/LPRest2003.pdf

Rytina, N. (2006). *Estimates of the Legal Permanent Resident Population and Population Eligible to Naturalize in 2004.* http://www.uscis.gov/graphics/shared/statistics/publications/LPRest2004.pdf

Rytina, N. (2007). *Estimates of the legal permanent resident population in 2006.* Washington, DC: Department of Homeland Security, Office of Immigration Statistics

Schmidley, A. D. (2001). Profile of the foreign-born population in the United States: 2000. Current Populations Reports, Special Studies, P23-206. Washington, DC: U.S. Census Bureau. Retrieved April 2008 from http://www.census.gov/prod/2002pubs/p23-206.pdf

Schmidley, A. D., & Robinson, J. G. (2003). Measuring the foreign-born population in the United States with the current population survey: 1994–2002. Population Division Working Paper No. 73. Washington DC: U.S. Census Bureau

Shryock, H. (1938). Methods of estimating post-censal population. *American Journal of Public Health, 28*, 1042–1047

Shryock, H., & Lawrence, N. (1949). The current status of state and local population estimates in the Census Bureau. *Journal of the American Statistical Association, 44*(246), 157–173.

Siegel, J. (2002). *Applied demography: Applications to business, government, law, and public policy.* San Diego: Academic Press

Skeldon, R. (1987). Migration and the population census in Asia and the Pacific: Issues, questions and debate. *International Migration Review, 21*(4), 1074–1100

Smith, S., House, M. (2004). "Temporary Migration Flows in Florida." Presented at the annual meeting of the Southern Demographic Association, October 14-16, Hilton Head, SC

Smith, S. K., Tayman, J., & Swanson, D. (2001). *State and Local Population Projections: Methodology and Analysis.* New York: Kluwer Academic/Plenum Publishers.

State of Minnesota (2005). *The Impact of Illegal Immigration on Minnesota: Costs and Population Trends.* St. Paul: Office of Strategic Planning and Results Management, Minnesota Department of Administration. Retrieved May 2008 from http://www.state.mn.us/mn/externalDocs/Administration/Report_The_Impact_of_Illegal_Immigration_on_Minnesota_120805035315_Illegal%20Immigration%20Brief%2026.pdf

Statistics Finland. (2004). *Use of registers and administrative data sources for statistical purposes: Best practices of statistics Finland.* Helsinki: The Author.

Stigler, S. (1986). *The history of statistics: The measurement of uncertainty before* 1990. Cambridge: Belknap Press of Harvard University Press

Swanson, D. (1986). Evaluating Population Estimates and Short-Term Forecasts. Applied Demography 2 (November): 5-6.

Swanson, D. (1989). Confidence Intervals for Post-censal Population Estimates: A Case Study for Local Areas. *Survey Methodology, 15*, 271–280.

Swanson, D. (2004). Advancing Methodological Knowledge within State and Local Demography: A Case Study. *Population Research and Policy Review, 23*(4), 379–398.

Swanson, D., & Hough, G. (2007). An evaluation of persons per household (PPH) data generated by the American community survey: A demographic perspective. Paper presented at the annual meeting of the Southern Demographic Association, Birmingham. Retrieved October 2008 from http://www.census.gov/acs/www/AdvMeth/Multi_Year_Estimates/presentations.html

Swanson, D., & Pol, L. (2005). Contemporary developments in applied demography within the United States. *Journal of Applied Sociology, 21*(2), 26–56

Swanson, D., & Pol, L. (2008). Applied demography: Its business and public sector components. In Y. Zeng (Ed.), *The encyclopedia of life support systems, demography volume.* Oxford: UNESCO-EOLSS Publishers (with L. Pol). http://www.eolss.net/

Swanson, D., & Tayman, J. (1995). Between a rock and a hard place: The evaluation of demographic forecasts. *Population Research and Policy Review, 14*, 233–249

Thorvaldsen, G. (2006). Away on census day: Enumerating the temporarily present or absent. *Historical Methods, 39*(2), 82–96

United Nations (1969). Methodology and evaluation of population registers and similar systems. Studies in methods (no. 15). Sales no. E.69.XVII.15. New York City: United Nations

U. S. GAO. (1993). *Illegal Aliens: Despite Data Limitations, Current Methods Provide Better Population Estimates. GAO/PEMD-93–25*. Washington, DC: United States General Accounting Office.

U. S. GAO. (1999). *Survey Methodology: An Innovative Technique for Estimating Sensitive Survey Items. GAO/GGD-00–30*. Washington, DC: United States General Accountability Office.

U. S. GAO. (2006). *Social Security Administration: Procedures for Issuing Numbers and benefits to the Foreign-Born. GAO-06–253T*. Washington, DC: United States General Accountability Office.

Van Hook, J., Bean, F. (1998). Estimating unauthorized Mexican migration to the United States: Issues and results. U.S. Commission on Immigration Reform, Binational Research Papers. Retrieved January 2008 from http://www.utexas.edu/lbj/uscir/binpap-v.html

Van Hook, J., Zhang, W., Bean, F., & Passel, J. (2006). Foreign-born emigration: A new approach and estimates based on matched CPS files. *Demography*, *43*, 361–382

Walashek, P., & Swanson, D. (2006). The roots of conflicts over US census counts in the late 20th century and prospects for the 21st century. *Journal of Economic and Social Measurement*, *31*(3, 4), 185–206

Walsh, J. (2007). Illegal aliens: Counting the uncountable. *The Social Contract* (4): 216–223. Retrieved April 2008 from http://www.thesocialcontract.com/artman2/publish/tsc_17_4/index.shtml

Warren, R. (1982). Estimation of the Size of the Illegal Alien Population in the United States. Paper presented at the Annual Meeting of the Population Association of America, San Diego, CA.

Warren, R., & Passel, J. (1987). A count of the uncountable: Estimates of unauthorized aliens counted in the 1980 census. *Demography*, *24*(3), 375–393.

Williams, B., Nichols, J., & Conroy, M. (2002). *Analysis and management of animal populations: Modeling, estimation, and decision making*. San Diego: Academic Press

Wolter, K. (1986). A combined coverage error model for individuals and housing units. SRD Research Report Number: Census/SRD/RR-86127. Washington, DC: U.S. Bureau of the Census

Wolter, K. (1990). Capture–recapture estimation in the presence of a known sex ratio. *Biometrics*, *46*(1), 157–162

Woodrow, K. (1990). Using census and survey data to measure unauthorized immigration and emigration from the United States. *Statistical Journal of the United Nations Economic Commission for Europe*, *7*, 241–251

Woodrow-Lafield, K. (1995). An analysis of net immigration in census coverage evaluation. *Population Research and Policy Review*, *14*(2), 173–204

Woodrow-Lafield, K. (1998). Unauthorized Residents in the United States in 1990: Issues of Uncertainty in Quantification. *International Migration Review, 32*(1), 145–174.